In memory of all those brave men and horses who fought and died in the Middle East a century ago.
And with gratitude to the many people who helped me, especially the hospitable horsemen and women,
during my journey through Israel. God bless you - Shéhashem yevarech etchem.

Edited by Jonathan Constant
Proofed by Jonathan and Marian Constant
Proofed (Israel) by Sharon Keinan
Maps by Peter Hall

Riding by Faith Through
ISRAEL

Tracey Elliot-Reep

TRACEY ELLIOT-REEP

Published by Tracey Elliot-Reep 2018
Text and photographs © Tracey Elliot-Reep
Widecombe in the Moor,
Dartmoor, Devon TQ13 7TL,
England
www.traceyelliotreep.com

ISBN 978-1-905162-41-3

Contents

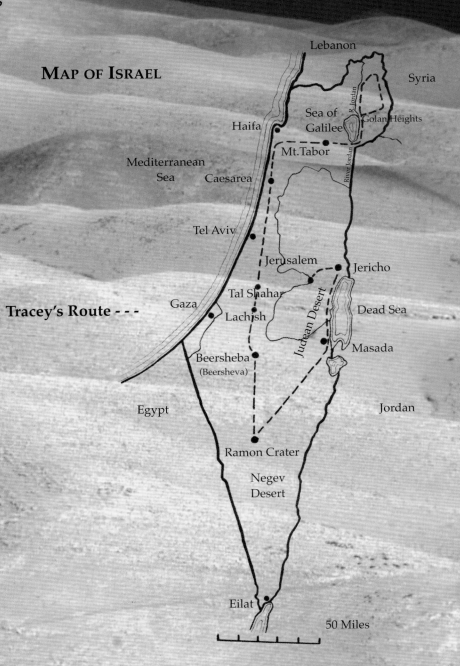

Map of Israel

Tracey's Route - - -

Lebanon

Syria

R. Jordan

Sea of Galilee

Golan Heights

Haifa

Mt. Tabor

River Jordan

Mediterranean Sea

Caesarea

Tel Aviv

Jerusalem

Jericho

Tal Shahar

Gaza

Lachish

Judean Desert

Dead Sea

Beersheba (Beersheva)

Masada

Egypt

Jordan

Ramon Crater

Negev Desert

Eilat

50 Miles

"The last and greatest cavalry charge in history." - General Allenby

"At a mile distance their thousand hooves were shattering thunder coming at a rate that frightened a man.
They were an awe inspiring sight, galloping through the red haze, knee to knee and horse to horse,
the dying sun glistening on bayonet points."
- Ion Idriess.

Foreword

A few years ago, while travelling in New Zealand, I was given a children's book called 'Brave Bess and the Anzac horses'. The story captured my heart and opened my eyes to the price paid by men and their horses in the battle to liberate Palestine. Until that moment, I'd been unaware of the bravery of the ANZAC (Australian and New Zealand) and British cavalry who, alongside other British allies, ended four centuries of Turkish rule in the Holy Land.

I was just 18 when I first visited Israel. I'd just finished a summer job in a circus, travelling across the south of England, and didn't want to spend a cold, wet winter in England, so I volunteered to work on a kibbutz in Israel. I found myself at Kibbutz Alumot overlooking the Sea of Galilee.

In a kibbutz, you earn your keep (board and lodging), so I used my art experience to help make biblical figures for tourists. It was very easy work, but I soon got bored with sitting down, so I went to milk the cows. They needed milking three times every 24 hours, and munched their way through a mountain of grapefruits. I shared a little room with another girl, but she left because I talked in my sleep!

I earned myself a few days off to go and visit other places in Israel. My elder sister Nicky had given me an address of some American friends in Jerusalem, who said I was welcome to visit them. I set off with a female friend, and we decided to hitch hike, but found ourselves stranded by an empty road as it was getting dark. I knew this wasn't safe, so I made a suggestion: "Let's try praying for a good lift, and no hassles all the way to Jerusalem."

In a short while a mini bus pulled over, full of soldiers, who spoke English and were so polite. After a two-hour drive, they delivered us right to my sister's American friends' doorstep. It was there in Jerusalem, sitting on their balcony, that I asked Jesus into my life to be my Lord and Saviour.

I knew I was meant to return as a photographer to ride horses around Israel. I would ask God occasionally as the years went by, "is it this or next year in Jerusalem?" And then suddenly I heard that the ANZAC re-enactment was to be at the end of October. I knew this was the time to go!

1. The ANZACs ~ Charge of Beersheba

From a speech by Israeli Prime Minister Benjamin Netanyahu:

"Nearly 4,000 years ago, Abraham came to Beersheva, the city of seven wells. Exactly 100 years ago, brave ANZACs (soldiers in the Australian and New Zealand Army Corps (1914-18)) liberated Beersheva for the sons and daughters of Abraham and opened the gateway for the Jewish people to re-enter the stage of history. The heroism of your fallen men will never be forgotten, liberating the Holy Land, and ending 400 years of Ottoman rule in one great dash. The horses were as legendary as those who rode them. Their sacrifice was a step to the creation of Israel."

"The horses were as legendary as those who rode them."
Prime minister Benjamin Netanyahu

"ANZAC soldiers who went on to capture Jerusalem, Tiberias, Megiddo and northwards were actually retracing the footsteps of the heroes of the Bible. They were stepping on the verses of the Bible and they knew it.

"It stood as a shining example for us. It was an example of a spirit of fortitude and courage and the willingness to act in defence of our people and our values. We saw 800 cavalry go against 4,000 embedded Turks with machine guns in bunkers. The few won against the many. That is the spirit of the army of Israel."

Beersheba is surrounded by desert to the south and to the east, and the Turkish forces expected it to be impassable. However, most of the horsemen set out late in the afternoon on 28 October 1917, and crossed the desert under cover of darkness. They rode quietly in fours, brigade after brigade, in a column more than nine miles (15km) long. On the third night they made a 28 mile (45km) trek and at dawn all the columns of mounted troops met near Beersheba.

There had been two failed attempts to break through the Turkish /German defensive line between Gaza on the coast and Beersheba 27 miles (43km) inland, leading to the death of 10,000 Allied soldiers. General Allenby, the newly appointed commander of the Egyptian Expeditionary Force, decided to try an outflanking manoeuvre via Beersheba, and attack the trenches protecting Gaza from behind.

It was said that a British officer had deliberately dropped a note saying an attack on Beersheba was impossible due to a lack of water, this had been picked up by Turkish forces, and as a result, the area was relatively lightly defended. So ANZAC General Sir Harry Chauvel (later to become one of Australia's most celebrated generals) hatched a daredevil plan for the ANZACs to attack Beersheba from the east.

One of the modern-day Australian riders who I met there, Beth, sketched out their route for me and described the challenge they faced: "Forty-eight hours without water, travelling by night with British yeomen support, to avoid being spotted by German aircraft."

On the morning of October 31, two infantry divisions launched a frontal assault on Beersheba, while the ANZAC horsemen, with British foot soldiers in reserve, went into action against the Turkish positions at the back of the town, catching them by surprise.

Before mounted troops could approach the town itself, a large hill called Tel el Saba first needed to be taken. This overlooked the plain in front of Beersheba, and machine gun positions would have mown down the horsemen in minutes. So the New Zealand Mounted Rifles attacked the hill, which was well defended by 300 Turkish troops, and it took nearly six hours of fighting, with many casualties, before they managed to capture the first enemy position. Two or three machine guns were taken, and were turned on the enemy. The 'Aucklands', as they were known, were joined by the Wellington Mounted Rifles, who charged up the hill on foot.

In was almost dusk by the time the hill was taken, and the ANZACs were running out of time to attack Beersheba and capture its wells – these were crucial for their many horses, which had been without water for 48 hours and would die of thirst.

Beth Clarke sketched on a piece of paper the route the ANZACs with British yeoman took from Gaza.

Photographs below were taken by Jim Wallace in 1917

Captured enemy artillery at Beersheba

"On our way to Jerusalem"

4th Auckland Mounted Rifles north of Beersheba

James (Jim) Wallace Watson achieved the rank of 2nd Lieutenant and was awarded the Military Medal in 1918 "for acts of gallantry and devotion in the field."

Jim Wallace Watson served in the Auckland Mounted Rifles, which captured the Tel el Saba stronghold, making it possible for the Australian Light Horse to attack Beersheba. His niece Trina Shaw told me some of his story.

Jim was born in Scotland in 1894 and travelled to New Zealand at the age of 14. He spent five years at war in the Middle East and took part in the Gallipoli Campaign, including the costly battle at Chunak Bair. Jim wrote in his diary on 30th August 1915: "We gained about 400 acres in four days fighting; 1,000 men killed and wounded. Land is very dear here."

After Gallipoli, he returned to Cairo and Palestine, and with the Auckland Mounted Rifles he supported the Australian Light Horse assault on Beersheba. Afterwards they pressed on towards Jerusalem and then Jaffa. He was badly wounded at the battle of Ayun Kara in November 1917, just a few days before Jaffa was taken.

"The mounted rifles were not cavalry," Trina told me. "They rode to a battle, then dismounted and fought on foot. The unit was broken up into groups of four men. One would hold the horses, while the others fought."

She continued: "Keeping the horses fed and watered was a real challenge while travelling through Palestine. Thousands of horses were brought here from New Zealand, but at the war's end, only about four horses were brought home. Some were sent to France to be used in the fighting there. But Jim, like many of the men, shot his horse rather than have him sold or given to the locals. They knew that they would end up pulling carts, and didn't wanted their horses to be mistreated."

Map of Israel

Lebanon
Syria
Mediterranean Sea
Haifa
Jordan River
Tel Aviv
Jericho
Jerusalem
Gaza
Dead Sea
Beersheba
Egypt
Negev Desert
Eilat
50 Miles

Beersheba
Tel el Saba
A
A
A
A
A
A

Tracey's Route - - -   **ANZAC Route .... A**

Ernest Pauls' tent; (top) in Beersheba after the charge.

Catherine Stedman and Ernest Pauls, who was awarded the 1914/5 Star, British War Medal, Victory Medal & ANZAC Commemorative Medallion.

I met Catherine Stedman who was riding with her cousin Rob Unicomb. She told me her grandfather Ernest Pauls had taken part in the Charge of Beersheba and sent me his comprehensive diary. This was what he wrote the day after the charge on the 1 November 1917:

"Came once again through Battle safely. One of the most magnificent mounted charges ever made in history by Australian Mounted troops resulting in the capture of Beersheba and the whole of its garrison and guns and munitions. At mid day yesterday we were well under cover. We got orders to unsaddle and feed up. We then had a much needed rest. At 4.10 pm we saddled up and received orders to secure tightly all gear to saddles. As we were going to gallop right through the Turkish defences, first stop at town of Beersheeba.

"We lined up behind a set of hills and came out at the gallop. We had 5 miles to go into town. At about 3 miles we came upon the Turks' first line. Two lines of our men went straight on and the third line took up a dismounted assault on the front line defences. Half an hour after the commencement we were right into Beersheeba rounding up large bodies of prisoners, guns etc. "Shock action" they call these tactics and very successful as the enemy was taken absolutely by surprise, as will be recognised by the fact that six of our troop captured a whole battery of field artillery. The 12th and 4th Regt. were the two Regts to enter Beersheeba. Our Regt. (about 150 strong) took over 800 prisoners alone.

"This is absolutely the greatest charge ever made in the history of the campaign in this front and will live in history forever. Sad to relate some of the best pals a man ever had went under. Poor old Kilpartick was fatally wounded early in the charge, as was Flood, Cotter, Cook, Bradbury, Charters, Neirgard, Coley, McClymont and a lot more in the enemy's first line. We met with very heavy fire, but onward our boys galloped over trenches and redoubts, making straight for Beersheeba, while those who had their horses shot from under them took up the attack on the redoubts."

"This is where we were met with such disastrous resistance. We galloped into action and dismounted our Hotchkiss about 20 yards from the enemy and by all rules of the game we should be dead now, but the dust from the galloping and yelling men was so thick, which enabled us to get the gun in so close. The yelling, surging, seething, galloping men of the 12th went straight on past each trench and into Beersheeba, capturing large forces before the enemy had time to realise we had attacked at all. Our men cleaned up the whole of the town and surrounding area of all prisoners, guns etc. The General staff had evacuated per train, but the 1st A.M.D, who were out on our right, succeeded in derailing their train and capturing the whole staff and 700 other prisoners, also smashing an armoured train."

The ANZACs

Riders had come from across Australia and New Zealand, many representing their ANZAC forefathers. Avon Moffatt, whose husband had been in the 12th Light Horse, was still riding at 82 years old. There were a handful of Aboriginal people, and I also met a soldier from the Australian army who hadn't ridden before!

"Would any person meet the other if they were not meant to?" asked Ihab Zeidan poetically. He was one of the Druze team looking after 100 horses and their riders – a popular figure, because he was always so cheerful and helpful. He helped me to get to the best place to photograph the practice charge, which was so exciting. There were so many ANZAC riders on their colourful horses in the billowing desert dust.

The Horses

During the First World War, more than eight million horses died, on both sides – mostly from Europe, the United States and Canada. With most major battles taking place on the Western Front, the hardships of the Middle East often go forgotten. In fact, more than 130,000 Australian and 10,000 New Zealand horses were shipped here, and only a few returned.

    The horses and their riders developed particularly strong bonds, each relying on the other to survive. Inevitably, many horses were killed beneath their riders, or men shot from the saddle, so those partnerships which survived became closer than ever. After the war, many soldiers asked to bring their beloved horses home, and some even offered to pay the army for them.

    Tragically, due to quarantine regulations and fear of disease, they had to be left behind. Younger horses were destined to be sold, and sick horses were put down. Some men tried to get their horses designated as sick, and when that failed, they would ask for a farewell ride. They would return on foot carrying their saddle and bridle, claiming their horse had slipped into a hole and broken a leg, so they had been forced to shoot it.

    I saw this poem on a billboard inspired by the feelings of the Australian Light Horse:

So farewell to the Yarraman old warhorse, farewell,
    Be you mulga bred chestnut or bay.
    If there's a hereafter for horses as well
    Then may we be with you some day.

Security forces were on every corner and in between. "If you hear a bomb, drop to the ground. Gaza regularly sends bombs over here," one of them told me. When Israel withdrew from the Gaza Strip in 2005, rockets were fired onto the towns of Ashdod and Beersheba. Necessity is the mother of invention, so the Israelis had to act quickly to protect their civilians. They created the so-called Iron Dome which is said to take down 90% of mortar shells seconds after they have launched, enabling Israelis and visitors to get on with their daily lives, even at times of high tension.

New Zealand, Australian and Israeli flags.

The practice charge in front of the Beersheba skyscrapers.

It was moving to see Israeli people shaking the Australians' hands and saying "thank you!" One of them even brought me a cup of coffee! I tried to get some close-up shots of a street parade, but was thrown out by security... so I hurried off to the park where the re-enactment charge was taking place. I stationed myself in a good position, with the consent of a policemen on a big Friesian horse, but a security guard later told me to go to the grandstand. Here I had to join a queue and pass through a security check, but eventually found a seat with a good viewpoint.

The packed, noisy grandstand was eagerly anticipating the re-enactment, but we had to wait because the Prime Minister was delayed. I was getting anxious as the sun was sinking, and casting long shadows – it was a perfect light to capture the charge. In the nick of time, a long line of black cars arrived and once the dignitaries were seated, the charge began... at a walk, but I could imagine them galloping through the dusk, as they had exactly 100 years ago. After the speeches, the horses moved back into the shadows... and then suddenly 20 ANZACS came charging back, much to the crowd's delight! Afterwards I remained seated for a while, deep in my thoughts, as the crowds dispersed.

For I am the Lord your God, the Holy One of Israel, your Saviour... Therefore I will give men for you, and people for your life.
Fear not, for I am with you; I will bring your descendants from the east, and gather you from the west; I will say to the north, give them up!
And to the south, do not keep them back! Bring my sons from afar, and my daughters from the ends of the earth.
A prophesy by Isaiah, 43:3-4 (around 750 BC)

During the First World War, more than 10,000 horses were shipped from New Zealand and over 130,000 from Australia – known as Walers because they came from New South Wales. They were descended from strong workhorses bred by the early colonists, who needed animals that would thrive in the Australian climate. So they shipped horses from the Cape of Good Hope, probably a breed called barbs, and many others from around the world, including thoroughbreds, Clydesdales, Suffolk Punch, Cleveland Bay, Lincolnshire Trotter, Norfolk Roadsters, Yorkshire Coaches, Timor ponies, Arabians, Percherons and more native British breeds. Cross breeding produced a versatile workhorse, which were good weight carriers and able to thrive in the tough environment. They were bred by the thousand on farms and stations across Australia, both for domestic use and for export, initially to the British Army in India. Strict standards of conformation and temperament were monitored by breeders on behalf of the fastidious Army Remount Service.

Walers were used overseas as remounts for the cavalry, as artillery horses, and as carriage and sport horses for both the British Army and the Raj in India. By the 1860s, the Waler was regarded by the British as one of the finest cavalry horses in the world.

After the First World War, a monument was erected in Sydney by returning soldiers who had to leave their mounts behind, bearing the inscription: "Erected by members of The Desert Mounted Corps and friends to the Gallant Horses who carried them over Sinai Desert into Palestine, 1915 – 1918. They suffered wounds thirst, hunger and weariness, almost beyond endurance but never failed. They did not come home. We will never forget them."

"The horses were as legendary as the men who rode them... One of the most bitter heartfelt stories of those old soldiers was of the fact that the horses did not come home." Australian Prime Minister Malcolm Turnbull

Australian Prime Minister Malcolm Turnbull said at the 100 year commemoration: "The Australian Light Horse were not meant to fight on horseback; they were mounted infantry and they were to ride to the battle, dismount, one man would hold the horses, three others would go in and fight like infantry. But on this occasion, water was short, they had no choice. General Harry Chauvel ordered that afternoon that they had to charge and he said: "Put Grant straight at it." What William Grant and the men of the 4th and 12th Light Horse Regiments achieved that day was astonishing. They charged six kilometres into Turkish fire. Their determination was unstoppable."

"While those young men may not have foreseen, no doubt did not foresee, the extraordinary success of the State of Israel, its foundations, its resilience, its determination, its indomitability against overwhelming odds, their spirit was the same. Like the State of Israel has done ever since, they defied history, they made history and with their courage they fulfilled history."

Map of Israel

Lebanon

Syria

Jordan River

Mediterranean
Sea

Haifa

Sea of
Galilee

Golan Heights

Caesarea

Tracey's Route - - -

Tel Aviv

Jericho

Jerusalem

Gaza

Tal Shahar

Dead Sea

Lachish

Masada

Beersheba
(Beersheva)

Egypt

Ramon Crater

Jordan

Negev
Desert

Eilat

50 Miles

2. MY START

It was October 2017 and I was on my way to photograph the ANZAC centenary, but also to fulfil a long held dream to ride horses around Israel from the north to the south. My goal was to visit the Sea of Galilee, and to finish my ride in Jerusalem exactly 100 years after Lord Allenby and the Allies marked the liberation of Jerusalem after 400 years of Turkish rule.

A very good friend of mine, who had taught in a school in Israel, put me in touch with a horseman in the Negev desert. He, in turn, put me in touch with some people who were prepared to hire me their horses. There were two available: Zorg was a greying Paint Horse and Sussita was a palomino. They hadn't been ridden for several years, so I took them out around the Moshav area every day, but Zorg shied at anything spooky and it was a struggle to get them past some spots.

The family who rented the horses lent me their tack and helped me get the extra pieces of equipment I needed. During my last journey across Southern Europe, customs officials in Athens had seized my pack saddle and wouldn't let it go. So this time I took it with me, stuffing it into an oversized suitcase along with other saddlery equipment!

"We are a thirsty country with not a lot of water," remarked Amir the horse transporter, as we crossed the sun-scorched landscape. I braced myself. It was going to be a difficult challenge to find water for the horses in world as dry as this.

Faith doesn't make things easy - it makes them possible

Zorg and Sussita at Yehudia Ranch above the Sea of Galilee.

3. THE GOLAN HEIGHTS

"You can't do anything without horses here," commented Avishay, horseman on the Yehudia Ranch – one of the biggest private ranches in Israel, spread across 27,000 dunam (more than 6,600 acres) in the Golan Heights. "It's hard work and not well paid, so you have to love it!"

The distant views reminded me of my travels through Tanzania in Africa, although this part of northern Israel was far rockier. A sea of jagged stones covered the landscape, interspersed with small scrub trees. It was hard to imagine how the 1,000 breeding cows on the ranch could live off such terrain.

The Yehudia Ranch was owned by the three Giv'on brothers. Avishay introduced me to two of them, Shay and Yohay, who were inseminating cows using sperm from an Angus bull in Canada. "His name is Grand Slam," one of them told me. Avishay explained that although they have about 40 Simmental and Charolais bulls on the ranch, they still import new genes from top class bulls in Canada, as mixed breeding makes the herds much stronger.

"There are 250 ranches in Israel, mainly in the north," Avishay continued. "Israel is a pretty costly country, and rearing cattle is very expensive. When they import cheap meat from abroad, it makes it difficult for Israel ranches."

As Avishay continued to show me the horses and foals, we passed a dead wolf lying bloated in the yard.

"Wolves are a very big problem here on the Golan," he said. "Yesterday eight wolves came to the calf pen. We had to shoot one, and the others scattered. Both wolves and jackals kill and eat new born calves, even when the cow is still giving birth. Some of our cattle also get stolen – the trouble is, the ranch is so big we can't watch it all.

"It's the end of the dry season and we are desperate for rain. It's getting later and later each year," added Avishay, before dashing off on his horse, which nimbly skimmed across the rocks. Dartmoor, where I live, is considered rocky, but this was extreme!

"For He orders His angels to protect you wherever you go.
They will hold you with their hands to keep you from striking your foot on a stone...
The Lord says, "I will rescue those who love me, I will protect those who trust in My name." Psalm 91:10-14

That night, as I lay in my sleeping bag on the floor of an old Syrian army outpost, I could hear the jackals yapping noisily. It made me think of the dangers which lay ahead. I was grateful for God's protection

Right from the start, everything had been expensive – from renting the horses, to buying equipment, to transportation. I was wondering how I was going to make my budget stretch enough to complete the journey. That was until I asked Ofer Grinshpah how much I owed him after, with much patience, he had managed to put shoes on Sussita's hinds, which the previous farrier had refused to touch. "I'm glad to help," Ofer said with a smile, "it's my contribution!"

Apparently Sussita had a bad reputation, and confirmed this as we battled with her halter. I was quickly learning about the horses' characters. When I first saw her, I noticed she had a swollen eye, as if she'd had a nasty bump, as well as a strange lump on her neck – I asked the owners about these but got no reply. I soon discovered she had a bad habit of flinging herself backwards, often breaking the headcollar or bridle.

Ofer told me how he became a farrier. "I was working on a ranch in Nebraska, USA, and wanted to know how to put shoes on my own horse. It was thirty below freezing and keeping close to the forge also helped me to keep warm!"

He preferred work as a farrier to competition riding. "People ride to win in competitions, and you have to get the horse to give you 110 per cent. I am more of a cowboy. I'm quite happy with my choice!"

Above right: Avishay, Ofer and Durien checking my route on the map.
Above left: Ofer Grinshpah putting hind shoes on Sussita.

We studied the maps together, but the names were in Hebrew, so I didn't have a clue! Avishay marked an enclosure where the horses would be secure on the first night, and advised me to leave early. But as usual when I start a new journey, it took time to pack up and get the panniers balanced. When we did eventually leave, it was slow going, as we picked our way through the rocky terrain and tall, dry grasses.

I was accompanied by a young man, who was spending the first week with me. He had been in the army, so could read maps, but made me uneasy. However, I ignored my gut instincts – agreeing with others that in a country of unrest, two people were safer than one.

Along the way the horses pricked their ears at the wild pigs, who grunted and rushed off in their family groups. We passed several burnt out tanks from the Yom Kippur War, which began in 1973, when a coalition of Arab States crossed ceasefire lines and made a surprise attack. In all, 80,000 Egyptians crossed the Suez Canal and advanced virtually unopposed into the Sinai Peninsula in the south, while in the north, 1,500 Syrian tanks moved into Israel across the Golan Heights, opposed by just 400 Israeli tanks.

Caught off-guard, Israel took three days to mobilise its forces. After three days of fierce fighting on the Golan, all the Syrian tanks were destroyed. Meanwhile, the Israeli army launched a counter attack and pushed the Egyptians and Syrians back to pre-war ceasefire lines.

As I rode over the battlefield, amid the carnage of destroyed tanks, I could only imagine how terrifying it must have been to face this onslaught.

Yom Kippur War

The Egyptians and Syrians were determined to regain the territory they had lost in the Six Day War of 1967, which came about when the Soviet Union incorrectly told the Syrian government that Israeli forces were massing in northern Israel to attack – although clashes between Israel and Syria had been escalating for about a year.

Syria was in coalition with Egypt, whose President asked the United Nations Emergency Forces, stationed between Israel and Egypt, to evacuate their positions. Egypt then moved troops into the Sinai Peninsula bordering Israel, occupied Sharm al-Shaykh on the southern tip of the Sinai Peninsula, and blockaded the Israeli port of Eilat on the Gulf of Acquba, arguing that access to Eilat was through Egyptian territorial waters.

This was a dangerous threat to Israel, which attacked Egypt and Syria, destroying their air forces on the ground. Jordan also joined the war, attacking Israel. During this Six Day War, all the countries which fought Israel ended up losing land. Israel captured the West Bank from Jordan, the Gaza Strip and the Sinai Peninsula from Egypt and the Golan Heights from Syria.

Even though my companion was map reading, we had to backtrack a few times when the tracks petered out into thick bush. Darkness engulfed us as early as 5 o'clock, so I offered him my torch, but he refused. I followed him through tall, spiky vegetation into an abandoned Syrian settlement consisting of broken down walls and deep pits, which looked like shell craters. I was worried that the horses might fall in. They were not used to scrambling over sharp, rocky ground, and it was even harder in the dark. We continually bashed our legs, and the sharp thistles made my bruised legs feel like pin cushions.

It seemed like we went to and fro for hours, until the young man led us to a padlocked gate. He did a good job of unpicking the barbed wire fence, and putting it back together again once we were through. At last we arrived at the fenced area, where Avishay and Durien had kindly left a big pile of oat hay for the horses and water for us. It was a relief to see a pool of water where the horses could drink.

The young man slept by the fire, while I slept in my tent. I could hear the horses clattering over the rocks, as they moved around the enclosure, sniffing out the grain which was hidden in my tent. I continually punched the tent roof to keep them away, worried that they would trip over the tent strings.

Syrian Border

Early the next morning I tied up the horses and gave them the grain they had been searching for throughout the night. Sussita immediately pulled back and broke the lead rope, which I knotted before saddling up the horses. My companion tried to help, but didn't take it well when I said he hadn't put the breastplate on correctly.

He had been at a loose end, and could read maps, so I'd been willing to give him a week to prove himself. We originally intended to hire another horse, but only had one riding horse and one pack horse, so we had to take turns riding and walking. I was having serious doubts about his attitude. He was so negative about everything, and I was feeling the strain.

At one point, when I was walking and he was following on horseback, with headphones in his ears, I turned round to find he had vanished. After waiting for ten minutes, I retraced my steps and found him trying to secure a loose pack.

I did it for him, and we carried on… but we suddenly found ourselves at the Syrian border – over six miles off our route. I'd wanted to give the horses an easy first day, as they weren't very fit. Neither was my companion, whose energy was flagging, and who stamped on all my suggestions as we looked for water. I'd had enough. I stated, firmly: "This is not going to work."

Can two walk together unless they be agreed? Amos 3v3

"I will leave you then," he said threateningly.

"Okay, go ahead," I replied. He hadn't expected that, thinking I would beg him to stay! He flew into a tantrum, firing a volley of complaints at me... how I neglected the horses... how it wasn't his fault that we'd ended up on the Syrian border.

"I never said it was," I replied calmly, "why don't you just stop talking." But this didn't stop the flood of complaints…

"I was wary of you when you first came with a bunch of money to hire the horses… I don't even fancy you!" (What a relief. He was young enough to be my son!). "I care about these horses, but not about you." It was f'ing this and f'ing that as he threw the map on the ground and wrenched his bag out of one of the panniers, scattering the contents all over the ground and causing Sussita to stagger slightly as packs on her back went lop-sided.

"I hope your God looks after you!" he jeered sarcastically, as he marched off up the road with his thumb out.

"Amen" I replied, knowing that my good God would, as He had given me this assignment and as in all my other journeys as a photojournalist, both on and off horses, He and His team of angels had taken care of me. After taking a moment to recover from his angry outburst, I took a big breath and whispered, "so what's the plan now God?"

Having repacked the panniers, I picked up the Hebrew map and tried to work out where we were and where I could find water for the horses. I could see some lakes to the east, but there seemed to be several barbed wire fences, with no obvious gateways, standing in our way.

I took a deep breath and decided to head for the Golan Heights trail, where I soon saw cattle. "There must be water around here!" I told myself.

I spotted a pipeline, and followed it to a large, circular water trough, where the horses enjoyed a welcome drink. I did consider camping here, but we would be very obvious out in the open, and I was worried it wouldn't be safe.

After one more drink, we followed the marked Golan trail upwards, past scattered cows and calves and through the oak scrub. I was grateful to be alone and it felt so peaceful, apart from a noisy pack of yapping jackals and a family of grunting wild pigs who crossed the track. But I was also conscious that it would soon be dark. We needed to use this short period of beautiful light to find a secure, hidden place to camp.

I tried to get into a fortified kibbutz, but the only unlocked gate wasn't wide or tall enough for the horses. As the light faded I quickly made a U-turn back into a military zone, ignoring a sign that warned against entering after sundown. I found a spot hidden in the oak scrub, fed the horses and tethered them where they could eat grass amongst the rocks. I then cleared away the stones under the trees to pitch my small tent. The temperature plummeted as it got dark, and I pulled on more layers – the first time I had felt cold in Israel. I switched on my phone, and immediately it was ringing.

"How are you?" said an Israeli voice, in English.

"I'm fine, thank you," I replied, trying to work out who this could be, as no name had come up on the screen. Playing for time, I added: "How are you?"

"It's the police."

"Oh!" I exclaimed.

"Where are you?" he asked and mentioned the name of a kibbutz.

"That's probably where I am," I replied. "My map is in Hebrew!"

"Are you sure you are fine? Have your horses had water?"

"Thank you yes, and I am camping here peacefully with my horses. Everything is good!"

"Okay, but if you have any problems you can call 100, you know," he added kindly.

"Thank you, and thank you for calling," I replied, feeling relieved, but wondering who had reported me.

If it costs you your peace. It costs you too much. - Creflo Dollar

Let the peace from Christ rule (act as umpire continually) in your hearts,

(deciding and settling with finality all questions that arise in your minds).

Colossians 3: 15 Amp

The peace and quiet didn't last long. Suddenly, I heard heavy machine guns, interspersed with the sound of tanks rumbling by on a track just 50 metres away, causing the ground to vibrate – I hoped one wouldn't plough through my campsite. When they weren't making a racket, I was kept awake by yapping jackal and grunting wild boar. I was also cold. Here high up in the Golan, I needed to wear all my clothes just to stay warm.

Throughout the night I kept crawling out of the tent, moving the horses and tethering them, so they could graze a fresh patch of dried-up grass. I'd then hurry back and wriggle into my cosy sleeping bag. I lay there listening to the wildlife, and pondering my mistake of interrupting my sense of peace and giving an opportunity to the young man, who didn't have the attitude needed for this journey. In this instance, I decided, by pleasing people I had disobeyed God. When we come to the end of our lives and we stand before God, He's not going to ask us, "why didn't you please that person?" He's going to ask, "did you become the person I created you to be? Did you stay true to what I put in your heart?"

Camp spot on the Golan Heights

His mercies are new every morning. Great is His faithfulness – Lamentations 3v22

"There's a military base further up the mountain, maybe you can get water there?" said a couple, who were out for an early morning stroll. They had replied to my few disjointed words of Hebrew: "Boker Tov, sliha maim?" ("Good morning, excuse me... water?")

At the edge of the military base, a soldier kindly went to fill up the folding bucket that a friend had given me while riding through Italy. The young soldiers enjoyed our visit and took photos with their phones, before roaring off in their jeeps. I realised that these heavily armoured vehicles were the 'tanks' I had heard the previous night.

People were so generous in re-supplying my stock of grain, I was able to feed the horses three times a day.

This I declare of the Lord: He alone is my refuge, my place of safety, and I am trusting him. Psalm 91:2 NLT

It was a pretty ride, following the Golan Trail over the undulating countryside, through nature reserves dotted with young oak trees. I learnt that this used to be an ancient forest – one of the few in Israel – but the trees were cut down in 1903 to feed iron furnaces, used by the Turks to build a railway line from Istanbul to Mecca. Today, all trees are protected in Israel, and you need permission to cut down any tree whose trunk is more than 20cm wide (less than eight inches).

"Aren't you afraid to travel alone?" asked a woman in a group of walkers, heading in the opposite direction.

"I trust in God to look after me," I replied sincerely.

She turned to her fellow walkers and smiled. "I want to travel with her!"

Whenever I saw cattle, I got into the habit of keeping an eye open for water troughs. At one of these stops I realised with dismay that my precious canvas water bag had slipped out of my pack. I deliberated for a while about going back to look for it, and decided I had no choice – it was essential in this dry country. The bucket was the same colour as the landscape, so I prayed that I would spot it. When I dismounted to take a photo, I looked down and there it was, right at my feet!

Kibbutz Ein Zivan

In Israel, November days feel as warm as a British summer, so I was often caught out when it got dark at five. I was pushing on to find a good place to camp, when yet again a barbed wire fence stood in my way. As I tried to find a way around it, I rode directly into the entrance of Kibbutz Ein Zivan. I spotted some corrals, and hoped I could buy food and lodging for the horses.

The stables were deserted, so I led the horses around the kibbutz until I came across some teenagers. After a quick phone call, a patrol vehicle pulled up and I was taken to meet the stable manager, Uri, who offered me hay and grain for the horses. Then it was my turn: I found myself renting a lovely rustic room with its own veranda and shower – not what I am used to when camping on a budget! After several sleepless nights I was determined to savour every moment of comfort, and slept for nine hours! The following morning, after a big tasty breakfast in the kibbutz dining room, I went to find Uri at the stables.

"This is a common tea for Jewish and Arabic people – a middle Eastern remedy and a cure for everything from tummy ache to cancer," he said, offering me a cup of salva. As we chatted, some planes flew overhead.

Uri stopped in mid flow. "That can't be good."

"What?" I asked curiously.

"Usually no planes fly on a Saturday as it's the Shabbat." A few moments later we heard two bombs exploding. "There are three reasons why Israel attacks Syria: if they attack Israel or fire across the border; if the Iranians try to get advanced weapons to the Hezbollah in Lebanon; or if Hezbollah terrorists are becoming established at the base of the Golan."

"Before all the trouble started in 1982, Lebanon was a quiet country, with tourists visiting the beautiful beaches," Uri informed me. "That was until Syria invaded. Now the Hezbollah hold Lebanon hostage as they have more soldiers." (The Hezbollah are an extremist group, formed in Lebanon and intent on replacing Israel with an Islamic state).

"First I was a tank driver in the army, then a medic and now I rescue big tanks with tractors." The Israel Defense Force (IDF) requires the conscription of every 18-year-old man and woman – the men join for three years, the women for two. Some can defer service for voluntary work.

Uri continued: "Tourism is the main business in this kibbutz, although they also produce good wine and chocolate. There are many individual businesses here – one even makes buckets for apple picking, which are exported worldwide."

As we spoke, he kindly mended Sussita's bridle, which she had broken the previous day, by stepping on her reins as I tackled another barbed wire fence. When trying to get through a fence, I usually tied Zorg up rather than Sussita, as she had a habit of pulling back. I'd learnt to keep the cheek pieces loosely tied with a piece of leather, so they would undo rather than break.

Uri offered me some of his grain and made a phonecall to arrange for me to stay at Odem Moshav that evening.

There's an odd truth about our destination. It is this: the journey is actually our destination. We sometimes fall into the trap of wanting to arrive somewhere instead of living right where we are.
- Jill Austin

Zorg had a comfortable, forward-going stride, but he would frequently shy at anything unusual. I concluded that he must have impaired sight in his blue and white eyes – I had a horse in New Zealand who also shied a lot, and also had blue and white eyes. Zorg was a Paint Horse, although his black patches had now faded into white and could only be seen when I washed him down.

I was always be on high alert when travelling on the roads, anticipating anything he might consider scary. If I saw something flapping at the side of the road, or there was a scary vehicle approaching, I'd dismount quickly and hold his head. He was a very sociable, curious horse who would introduce himself to most other animals, apart from goats.

Sussita was altogether calmer, except when she was tied up. She was smaller and easier to pack up, whereas I had to be on tiptoes to lift and tie the pack on Zorg. The first time I did this, I held my breath – judging by the expression on his face, his giraffe-like high head carriage and his twitching ears, it looked like he might explode at any moment! I alternated riding the horses each day so the dead weight of the pack wouldn't cause saddle sores. The two of them were rather too closely related: Zorg was both Sussita's father and brother.

4. Mount Bental

At the base of Mount Bental I spied a water tap coming out of a rock. I never missed an opportunity to water my horses, so I refilled my Italian water bag several times, to allow them to have a good drink.

Halfway up the track to Mount Bental, Zorg stopped in his tracks transfixed by some figures descending towards us. I dismounted to let them go by, and so avoid an accident on the steep ascent, before continuing to the 3,842ft summit (1,171 metres). Mount Bental is one of the dormant volcanoes in a chain of mountains, which forms the border between Israel and Syria. At the top there was an Israeli IDF bunker built on older Syrian remains. I took my turn posing for a photo beside the signpost, and was surprised to see I was only 60km (37 miles) from Damascus in Syria.

Uri had advised me not to follow the Golan Trail off the mountain, as it was very steep and rocky, so instead I went back down the way I had come, before spending a frustrating hour riding around inside the perimeter security fence of Mount Bental Kibbutz, trying to find the exit. Eventually I found a gate on the south side, and turned north, in the opposite direction. The sinking sun was worrying me – I needed to get to Odem Moshav before the darkness caught up on us.

Syria to the East and the Mount Hermon range, and Lebanon to the north.

Zorg and Sussita on the border overlooking Syria.

Back on the Golan Trail, there were yet more time consuming wire fences to unpick, and then put back together again. I took to the road at one point, trotting to cover as much ground as possible, but it was too dangerous and stressful as the vehicles skimmed by. At any moment one of the horses could shy out into the path of a car.

So I turned off into the barren, rock-strewn moonscape, devoid of grass. Many hungry cattle stood around a water trough, so I offered the horses a drink, which they refused. With no time to waste, I pressed on, picking my way over the rocks. I was less than two miles (3km) from hay, water and security at Odem Moshav, but I couldn't find the wire gate, marked on the map. My heart sank. It was too dangerous to travel along a road in the dark, and I had to find somewhere secure for the night. Eventually I found a gateway and let myself into a grassy area, where I could hide the horses in amongst the pine trees and pitch my tent. I called Uri's contact, Amiti. He didn't speak English, but within minutes the phone rang.

"Are you okay?" someone asked, introducing himself as Nir, and telling me he worked at Amiti's deer park. "It's better not to travel in the dark. Are you somewhere safe?" I confirmed that I was. Although we were not protected by the floodlit high security fence of a kibbutz, I did feel safe as no one had seen us come off the road in the darkness.

"Okay, come for coffee in the morning and we'll give your horses hay!" he offered. His friendly voice had reassured me, as I tethered the horses on their long ropes to graze, and continued to move them to new patches throughout the evening. At one point Sussita got the rope caught around her hind leg and threw herself on the ground, but I thanked God she had landed on the soft pine needles, and not on the usual rocky terrain.

Throughout the night I heard machine guns and bombs exploding, just over the border in Syria. I was relieved to be in Israel, remembering Uri saying, "we are just on the border where the biggest war in the world is happening right now."

On our journey through the barren rock strewn landscape to Odem,
we were grateful to find water in a rusty old watering trough.

I packed up at first light while the horses were eating their grain. By seven we were back on the same road, and I found an open gateway – its wire gate lying on the ground. I saw horses inside, so I closed it behind us.

I pulled out my phone to tell Nir we were on our way, but even though I'd been careful to switch it off to preserve the battery, it had reverted to factory settings. Technology often frustrates me – I hardly ever use a mobile phone back home on Dartmoor, south west England, as we rarely get a signal there. However, in this country, with its many potential dangers, a phone was essential.

On entering Odem, the second highest town in Israel at 3,580 ft (1,090 metres), I asked for directions to the deer park and was relieved to be greeted by a smiling Nir. He gathered a big armful of hay for the horses while I had tea, and then fiddled with my phone. Simply by reinserting the battery, he got it working again.

"My boss, Amiti, is a deer expert," he informed me as he showed me the different breeds, and the Ibex goats, jumping off piles of rocks in their enclosures. He took me to a big room surrounded by trophy heads of deer and other animals, gazing down on us, and added: "He is living his dream having this zoo!"

While leaving the Moshav, a large herd of colourful goats passed in front of us, and I reached for my camera, in its bag slung over the front of the saddle. As I did so, I sensed Zorg having a bit of a meltdown at the sight. Dust had stopped the autofocus from working, so rather than manually focusing from the saddle, while holding two lively horses, I slipped off his back and took some photos from the ground. As the goats disappeared into the dry landscape, I wondered how animals, especially cattle, could survive here.

Descending through the haze, I spotted the sprawling medieval Muslim fortification of Nimrod Castle on the southern slopes of Mount Hermon. It was built to guard the major access routes and had been captured and occupied many times through the ages, including by the Mongols and Alexander the Great who had built a city below at Banias. We passed the eerie, deserted shells of concrete buildings, splattered with machine gun fire.

I dismounted when we reached the road, caught my sunglasses on the horn of my Western saddle and they snapped. A Texan friend had given them to me, so I was sad about this – it was incredible they had lasted ten years. More importantly, my sunglasses were essential to protect my eyes from the sun, and also the dust, which blows over from the desert countries of Jordan and Syrian. It had jammed my camera, and made all my photos look hazy.

My mourning over my broken sunglasses was interrupted by a family from Connecticut, outside an army barracks.

"It was in her heart to make Aliyah (immigration to Israel)," said the father, indicating his tall daughter, in her khaki uniform, who was stationed at the barracks. As we said goodbye, they gave me a bottle of water, and I was handed another by the driver of a car, as we descended into the valley.

I had planned to get to the kibbutz at the bottom to buy hay, but our path was blocked by the Bannias river, flowing through a deep ravine. The only way round it was along a dangerous narrow road, packed with tourist buses and trucks. I felt stuck, and prayed for direction, before deciding to head back to a yard where I had seen some horses eating a big round bale of hay. Perhaps the owner might be nearby and sell me some?

Just as I arrived, an Arab man pulled up in his van and realising my God given opportunity, I asked, "are these your horses?". He proudly confirmed they were, so I continued: "Do you have any hay I could buy?"

"Help yourself!" he said, and introduced himself as Colin. "There's water in the yard, and a place for you to camp," he added before driving off. As I was unpacking the horses, another man arrived, speaking on his phone. By his stance I guessed he must be the owner of the yard and was talking to Colin.

"Just make sure you open the gate in the morning, as all the cows come into the yard to eat," he cautioned.

I was grateful to have a secure overnight stop, with water and hay for the horses, despite two black, decomposing wild pig carcasses lying in the yard. I was dragging my pack upwind of the bodies, when another pick-up arrived. I ignored it, somehow hoping we wouldn't be noticed (I don't like people knowing where we were camping), but the driver turned out to be a local security man called Yossi.

"Call me if you have a problem," he said, handing me a piece of paper with his phone number, adding, "I have to go and sort out a problem. I look after several thousand cattle and because of the late rains they are desperate for grazing."

He returned several hours later and under torchlight we drank tea from his flask, while he marked his stables at the Gona Kibbutz on my map, suggesting I head there the next day. From the darkness of the yard I could see the valley below, lit up with a myriad of lights. He pointed out the lights of a Lebanese town, just over the border, which seemed so close. I asked him about the wolves and wild pig carcasses.

"I was in Lebanon, in the army," he said blankly, "I don't shoot anything anymore." Before leaving he warned me: "If you hear the wild pigs in the night, put your light on and make a noise."

We passed many landmine warning signs and kept carefully to the track.

An Israeli cowboy giving my horses water at a kibbutz.

That night, a gale force wind battered my tent, so I couldn't hear wild pigs trying to steal our food, and it ripped out the tent pegs that I had attempted to screw into the hard ground. I tried to weigh the guy ropes down with rocks, but they flew off. The tent was flapping madly, and the two guide strings that I had tied to the yard rails, plus the weight of my body, were the only things preventing it from being completely blown away.

The gale continued throughout the following day, blasting dust into my eyes and blowing my hat off my head, even when tied tightly under my chin. After chasing after it several times, I found the only solution was to clench the hat string tightly between my teeth, especially while passing between the minefields. I simply couldn't do without both my hat and sunglasses.

"Watch out for the landmines on the Golan!" I had been warned, as there are over a million of them in this intensely patrolled military zone. Many of the mines date back to the fifties and sixties, and they continue to be a danger today – indicated by red warning signs attached to the wire fences. Although this is deadly territory for humans, it provides a sanctuary for wildlife, especially wolves, making this a source of tension between farmers and naturalists.

As on all my riding journeys, I alternated riding and leading the horses. I fell over several times – I'd had no sleep the previous night and my diet of nuts and tinned tuna fish wasn't enough to sustain my energy. To make matters worse, my eyes were stinging from the irritating gritty dust. It made me think that this must be just a small taste of what the horsemen had experienced a century earlier, while fighting in this dusty country. And they certainly didn't have the benefit of luxury sunglasses!

Passing through a kibbutz I hailed a pick-up truck and asked them where I could get water for the horses. "Follow us. We're cowboys!" they said, did a U-turn, and led me back to a cattle shed. A Jewish man gave the horses water, while a darker man invited me in to eat. He opened a fridge and laid the contents on the table telling me to help myself. "I'm an Arab," he told me. "We work well together here."

Landmines

After we left, and followed the track along the west side of the valley, Zorg had a shying fit. I looked at the map and realised I had missed a turning across the fields which Yossi had marked for me, but instead of backtracking, I carried on. I assumed I'd be able to get into the valley further on, but I didn't reckon on every gate being firmly padlocked to deter cattle thieves.

I found a water trough covered in bees. Remembering that Zorg had been bitten on the nose by a snake in his hay, I tried to remove them, only to be stung myself – just another source of discomfort to add to the heat, the dust, and the frustration of finding our route continually blocked.

After retracing our steps several times, I followed another track praying it wouldn't lead us to yet another locked gate, and I was encouraged to find it led to a kibbutz. It was nearly five o'clock, so I hurried to get in before the security gates were locked for the night. I was so relieved to reach what I assumed was Yossi's kibbutz, and called him to get directions to his barn, but when I couldn't see what he was describing, I realised I must be at the wrong one.

A resident told me to cross the busy main road and go immediately left, which took me around several fish ponds and back to where I had started. It was almost dark and I was frustrated that I had wasted valuable daylight going around in circles. I asked some men who looked blankly at me until I said the name of the kibbutz, when they pointed me down the main road.

It was too dangerous in the dark, so I returned to the Kibbutz Lehavot Habashan, that I had I left 20 minutes earlier. I spoke again to Yossi, who put me in touch with his friend Tony, who managed the cattle yards there. I was surprised to meet an Englishman who had come out to Israel from Birmingham 40 years ago!

Seeing the pictures in his office I remarked, "you look like cowboys!"

"We are!" he replied. "We are Israeli cowboys!"

A war memorial with a shredded Syrian and Israeli flags flapping.

We followed an old trade route road from Bannias.

The Hula Valley

I left at daybreak the next morning and followed the banks of the Jordan, the country's main river, which flows through the Hula valley and irrigates this rich agricultural area. It was drained in the 1950s when it became a breeding ground for mosquitoes carrying malaria, but was later reflooded to save the endangered ecosystem.

Back in the 19th century, this was regarded as one of the finest hunting grounds in Syria, inhabited by panthers, leopards, bears, wild boar, wolves, foxes, jackals, hyenas, gazelle and otters. Today it is best known as a sanctuary for birdlife, especially those which migrate along the Syrian / African Rift Valley. Every year an estimated 500 million birds (no less than 390 species) pass through the Hula Valley, an area less than 20 square miles. They include pelicans, water fowl, birds of prey and song birds.

"You won't miss the cranes. There are currently 40,000 in the Hula valley!" I was told. Most of them come from Russia and stop over on their way to Africa. Some decide to spend the winter in Israel, encouraged by bird feeding stations, set up to prevent damage to the crops.

Bird enthusiasts come from all over the world to see this impressive sight. The Keren Kayemeth LeIsrael Jewish National Fund (KKL-JNF) is developing protection plans – encouraging some species that are at risk of extinction and bringing back other birds that once nested in the valley. Its projects include tree planting, bird ringing and providing nest boxes for barn owls. Voles cause great damage to crops, but a single family of barn owls can eat up to 3,500 of them a year. So the owls offer an alternative to pesticides and poisons and are another great attraction for visitors.

5. THE JORDAN RIVER

I enjoyed watching the birds as I continued along the banks of the Jordan, which runs into Lake Kinneret (also known as the Sea of Galilee) and then into the Dead Sea where it evaporates. I saw mallard ducks, coots, and others with bright flashes of vivid turquoise. Our presence alarmed some big water rats, which scuttled across the green carpeted banks and into the reeds edging the river. This was the first green grass that I had seen, and it was refreshing. But still without sunglasses, the bright, dusty haze was harsh on my eyes, so I kept my gaze on the soothing river, looking out for the birds swooping and paddling.

My tranquillity was interrupted by revving, racing Land Rovers, filled with screaming adults, who left me covered in a blanket of dust and gave me a sneezing fit. I was disappointed to see the rubbish that littered these beautiful riverbanks.

I pondered the Bible stories about this historic river. Joshua, having just taken over the leadership from Moses, was guiding the Israelites into the Promised Land (about 1400 BC). But the river was in flood, so the priests carrying the Ark stepped into the water, and the flow of the river stopped, enabling all the people to cross on dry land (Joshua, chapter 3). And, of course, this was the same river where Jesus was baptised by John the Baptist.

"Jesus himself was baptised, as he was praying the heavens opened, and the Holy Spirit descended on him in the form of a dove. And a voice from heaven said, "You are my beloved Son, and I am well pleased with you." (Gospel of Luke, chapter 3)

Facing it, always facing it. That's the way to get through. Face it. – Joseph Conrad

"If you can get here," Libby, the manager at Vered HaGalil, told me on the phone, "I have a room for you tonight and tomorrow." It was midday. We had already done more than 12 miles (20km) and judging by the map we had over 10 miles to go (17km). We usually covered about 12 to 15 miles in a single day (20km to 25km), but this was a great offer! Tempted by a secure rest, hay for the horses and a much needed shower for myself, I gathered my reins and urged the horses into a trot.

After several miles we had to cross a narrow bridge, crowded with traffic. My heart sank, as I loathed taking the horses on dangerous roads with little or no verge. But there was no alternative, and no use procrastinating. Praying for protection, I unpicked the wire fence and urged the horses onto the main road, only to retreat as a stream of big trucks and tour buses sped towards us. Once they had passed, I ventured out again, and marched up the road, leading the horses – stopping only to ask some Arabs, who were selling drinks, if there was an alternative to crossing the busy bridge. They shook their heads, so I hurried across with Sussita on the outside, but even she tensed up as the trucks rumbled by.

A young Arab man in a jeep pulled up alongside and I motioned to him to stay there, and protect us from the traffic. Once we were on the other side, he helped get the horses across the road and through a narrow wire gate next to a cattle grid. The ground on the other side had been washed away, so the horses had to leap across, and I flinched when the pack got caught and ripped on the barbed wire fence, but it was such a relief that we had made it across the bridge and were still alive!

Before leaving, the young Arab showed me some photos of his horses on his phone and gave me his number, although calling him would have been a challenge as neither of us spoke each other's language! I followed a gravel road for a short distance before reaching another cattle grid beside a little wire gateway – too narrow for Zorg the packhorse. I groaned, as unpacking and repacking used up vital time and energy, but I wanted my shower and good food and rest for the horses.

If the atmosphere hadn't been so hazy, I imagined it would have been a very scenic ride, with the Jordan flowing through the valley below. I passed a family of hyrax sunning themselves on some rocks, but I didn't tarry as I was conscious that darkness was approaching and I didn't want to travel across the rocky countryside in the dark.

I picked my way across the volcanic, rock-strewn landscape, following the landmarks and contours on my Hebrew map. It was dusk as I approached our destination, Vered HaGalil, only to find our route blocked by a substantial gate with a heavy duty chain and padlock. I called Durien, from the Yehudia ranch who worked at Vered HaGalil, who asked me to send her my location on WhatsApp.

"I have no idea how to do that!" I replied, feeling rather feeble, fumbling with my phone in the dark.

A man's voice came on the phone: "Describe where you are."

"I'm just over the hill to the north, at a padlocked gate," I replied.

"Well you have to get through the fence!" The man stated, in a matter-of-fact way.

"Ok." I took a breath, and leaving the horses tied to the locked gate in the dark, I went to investigate the fence. Using my torch, I didn't have to go far until I found where the barbed wire had previously been cut, so I undid it, got my horses through and then refixed it as many had done before me. We continued along a track which disappeared into the darkness.

"You need to keep the pylon on your right," said Durien. I could see its silhouette against the night sky, but led the horses into a bundle of loose barbed wire, which wrapped around Sussita's hind legs. "Jesus!" I prayed, hoping she wouldn't panic, as it could be disastrous. Soothing her, I carefully backed her out, and breathed a sigh of relief and thanks.

"Keep going," Durien told me, "I'll meet you at the gate." Here we exchanged hugs and she guided me through the long dry grass to the corrals. After feeding the horses, we settled down on the edge of a floodlit arena watching Avishay (from Yehudia Ranch) and his friends training their horses for the Extreme Cowboy competition. After my long-awaited shower, I flopped into a bed at midnight – so grateful to have arrived – and pondered Durien's comment: "We have to do these kind of things in the army. Sleep out, learn to shoot, walk for miles. But you choose to do it!"

Vered HaGalil – Rose of the Galilee

It was lovely to wake up at Vered HaGalil, a peaceful and beautiful ranch located on a hill overlooking the Sea of Galilee. I could imagine that on a clear, dust-free day the view of the Golan Heights, Capernaum and the Mount of the Beatitudes, would be amazing.

"The founder of this ranch would have loved you and what you are doing!" Libby the manager enthused when Durien introduced us the following morning. "Yehuda Avni loved horses, nature and people. He came from Chicago at 23 years old and met Yona his wife in Israel. They came here from a rose farm in the south in 1961 (Vered HaGalil means rose of Galilee) and after a lot of hard work, clearing the land of boulders and bush, they made their dream come true, providing a place for people to enjoy nature and horse rides."

Libby patiently showed me how to send my location on WhatsApp and even called the company in Tel Aviv which had sold me my internet package – I appreciated this so much. Meanwhile Ben, who worked with the horses, kindly took my dusty clothes to the laundry. I remarked on his clear English accent and he told me that his mother was from the Lake District and had come as a volunteer to work on a kibbutz where she met his father. There was such a variety of backgrounds here! Durien's family were from South Africa while Avishay's came from Yemen.

Mount of Beatitudes

The following day I rode the horses around the dry, sun-baked Mount of Beatitudes, one of the places in Galilee where Jesus gave a list of blessings known as the Beatitudes. Speaking to a large crowd, who had come from all over the country to hear him, he healed everyone who touched him and cast out many evil spirits.

He also gave the challenging instructions: "Love your enemies, bless those who curse you, be good to those who hate you, and pray for those who spitefully use you and persecute you. Do good to those who hate you. Pray for those who curse you..."

As I imagined sitting there on this hillside listening to Jesus, I spotted a tortoise in the shade of the stone I was sitting on!

6. Sea of Galilee (Lake Kinneret)

It was amazing to be riding along the shores of the Sea of Galilee, also known as Lake Kinneret, where most of Jesus' miracles took place. In his day, this was a major spice trade route from the east to western Europe.

The coming of Jesus was prophesied many times before he was born – his birth was foretold hundreds of years earlier by the prophet Isaiah (chapter 7:14, around 750 BC). "Therefore the Lord himself will give you a sign. The virgin will conceive and give birth to a son, and you will call him Immanuel!" Isaiah also spoke (Isaiah 35: 5-6) about his miraculous ministry: "The eyes of the blind be opened and the ears of the deaf unstopped. Then the lame will leap like a deer and the mute tongue shout for joy." Another prophet called Micah (around 704-696 BC) declared that he would be born in Bethlehem and have a miraculous ministry.

After Jesus was baptised in the River Jordan, he went into the wilderness and fasted for 40 days before entering his ministry, casting out demons and healing many people. Despite this and all his miracles, religious people hated him, because he didn't stick to all their rules, but the people loved him as he healed everyone who came to him.

One day, Jesus was teaching from Simon's boat to a crowd on the shore of the Kinneret / Galilee. Once he had finished speaking he told Simon Peter to take his boat into the deeper water, and to let down his nets as he would catch many fish. Simon replied that they had tried all night but hadn't caught a thing. But however illogical this appeared to be, he was willing to do what Jesus suggested. They caught so many fish, that they had to call those in another boat to come and help – what great payment for loaning a boat out to Jesus!

Initially Zorg and Sussita refused to go into the lake, but once they felt the refreshing water splashing up under their bellies they pricked their ears, relaxed and enjoyed it.

As I rode the horses on the edge of Lake Kinneret (Sea of Galilee) I thought about some of the other stories of Jesus – such as the time when he and his disciples were taking a boat across the lake. Jesus was sleeping when a dangerous storm swept in. His disciples panicked and woke Jesus, fearing they could drown. Jesus simply rebuked the storm and immediately the lake became calm. The men were astonished, saying, "who can this be, that even the winds and the sea obey him?"

Another time (John 6: 18), his disciples were rowing across the lake, heading for Capernaum, and saw Jesus walking over the water towards them. They were scared, but he said to them, "it is I. Do not be afraid." He entered the boat, and immediately the boat was on the shore (Luke 8: 26).

When Jesus stepped out, he was met by a man possessed by a demon, who fell down and cried out, "what have I to do with you, Jesus son of the most high God?" Jesus asked him his name. He replied "Legion", because so many demons had entered him. They begged Jesus not to command them to enter the abyss, but into a herd of pigs which were grazing on the mountainside. He cast them out, the demons entered the pigs, which ran down and were drowned in the lake.

Do not delay; the golden moments fly! ~ H W Longfellow

Uri Peleg - Ramot Ranch

When Uri Peleg arrived at the stables, I could see he was a popular man, as many staff gathered to greet him. He turned to me, smiled and shook my hand. "You've completed part of my dream!" he said. "I admire you for what you have done. I always dreamt of riding across America without using a bridle!"

Uri drove me and the horses to his place on the north west edge of the lake and told me his life story. He'd started riding after leaving the army at 21, began working with cattle, and found his own way to ride. Later, he built his ranch, way above Lake Kinneret, where he lived with his family, taught riding skills and developed a series of DVDs, which he generously gave me.

He explained some of his teaching methods. "You need to train both the horse and rider," he said. "If you only train the horse, the rider doesn't know the codes. Both horse and rider need to know the same body language, vocal order and legs. Before you even hold the reins, you need to build safe communications."

Uri had twice ridden across Israel without a bridle. "I did it with no head piece – my horse was completely naked from the cinch forwards. When you do it correctly, the horse comes to love it. It's important to hold the reins, but they prefer a touch in their ribs rather than in the soft tissues of their mouths. Just to prove it worked, I rode from Lebanon to Gaza Strip and from Lebanon to Eilat."

"People must have been amazed!" I exclaimed. He smiled. "I remember two soldiers having an argument about whether my horse was wearing a bridle or not! You can only do something like this with the right horse, and you need to build the codes so deep that it happens automatically."

We returned to the grand Canadian cedar log cabin where he and his wife Justine lived, perched on the mountain far above the lake.

"I am so disappointed for you," Uri remarked. "The view is usually so amazing, but there's too much dust." I could imagine why people loved coming up here to ride along the beautiful trail.

Uri told me about his country. "This land belongs to the state of Israel. Citizens can rent it, as long as you use it for the purpose you have agreed. For example, if you have enough cattle, you get to rent the grazing, which also helps prevent fires. As we are a small country we have more room to ride because the land is not privately owned. People don't pay for the land, only for the electric, water and other expenses."

Uri told me that Israel needed to be strong, as it was threatened by the seven Arab nations that surrounded it. "For 19 years the Syrians continually fired at us and lobbed bombs from the Golan Heights." He indicated the valley below: "The farmers down there had to work the land with armour-plated tractors, and some of the children grew up sleeping in bomb shelters. In 1967 Israel chased the Syrians off the Golan Heights and in 1973 they tried to return. That was the Yom Kippur War when 1,500 Syrian tanks came over the Golan Heights and 400 Israeli tanks fought them back."

Photographing Uri Peleg riding his bridleless horse at Ramot Ranch above Lake Kinneret (Sea of Galilee).

Uri continued: "If Israel stops controlling Judea, Samaria and the West Bank and allowed their independence, Hamas will take over. Always the most extreme take control."

He went over maps with me and told me to keep in touch, as he knew horse people all around the country. He'd been such a great support, even finding me an ideal location for some filming. I asked him how much I owed him for his wonderful help.

"Give me what you think and then I will give you back half!"

The horses liked it on Ramot Ranch and didn't want to load, but Uri was the expert and thanks to his technique, never again did I have a problem.

Kibbutz Degania B

After a filming session by Jay and his son Daniel Rawlings on the shores of Lake Kinneret, Uri dropped us off at Degania Beit, where Rauven Tzion washed my horses down at his self-built shower and stables. They had a Mexican appearance, with warm terracotta walls and decorative gates.

"I'm Mexican not Jewish," he confirmed. "My mother was a Jewish girl and brought me here when I was seven, in 1958, after her husband was killed by a car in LA." After washing the horses he secured them in a corral with a heavy duty padlock. I was getting used to this level of high security – each stable had a similar padlock. As I travelled through this country, I often heard stories of stolen horses, sheep and vehicles. It was a risky place, but I felt reassured that God and his angels were keeping me, in all my ways, and I prayed to be discerning about where to camp with my horses.

Rauven advised me to lock myself into the windowless tack room that night, which I found slightly claustrophobic after spending a week sleeping outside in the Golan Heights.

The neighbouring Kibbutz Degania Alef was one of the first to be established – back in 1920 – and I asked him about the old Syrian tank which sat outside. I learnt that when the Syrians came here in 1948, the Kibbutznics had no weapons, so they fought the tanks with homemade mortar bombs, which they dropped through the hatch.

"My stepfather lost his eye fighting off the Syrians," he stated. "I was in the mortar regiment. Most of them were killed fighting under Mount Hermon." Rauven paused. "Now I like a horse trip. I like to enjoy. I am not looking to toughen up." I couldn't even imagine how it would feel to be in a war, and see all your friends killed.

Rauven helped me saddle up early as the days were short. "Senorita," he addressed me with a smile, "do you have toilet paper?"

Return Ministries

But the Lord will have mercy on the descendants of Jacob. He will still choose Israel as his special people once again.
He will bring them back to settle once again in their own land.
And people from many different nations will come and join them and unite with the people of Israel.
Isaiah 14:1

Jay Rawlings, the film man who kindly lent me some sunglasses, put me in touch with Dean Bye, the director of Return Ministries in the adjacent settlement. He invited me to their Shabbat meal at the Bikat Kinarot Centre.

I arrived to find a crowd of many nationalities and ages, including Christians, Arabs and Jews. They were working together to renovate the buildings, and also supported Jewish immigrants, including teaching them the complex Hebrew language. After helping ourselves to plates of food, we all sat down at a long table. Before eating the delicious meal, they blessed the bread and wine in the Jewish tradition.

I was asked to drop by early the next morning, and was met by a handful of people who gave me a welcome cup of tea. Next to the Union Jack I prayed for my country and Israel and then they prayed for me.

"I've read your New Zealand book, and loved it!" said an enthusiastic man, who rushed over and introduced himself as Grant. He was a volunteer from New Zealand and was riding around Europe and Israel on his motorbike.

"Remember the phrase 'Lama lo'," he said. "It means why not!"

"That's a good one!" I laughed, as I loved New Zealand. I called over my shoulder as I rode out of the gate, "sounds just like a Kiwi expression!"

I crossed the Jordan, rode through a plantation, and continued westwards. I pondered some verses from the prophet Jeremiah (12v5) which Dean sent to my phone: "If you have raced with the men on foot and they have worn you out, how can you compete with horses? If you stumble in safe ground how will you manage in the thickets of the Jordan? You brothers, your own family, even they have betrayed you. They have raised a loud cry against you. Do not trust them, though they speak well of you."

Perched on the brow of a hill to the north was Kibbutz Alumot. I had volunteered here when I first came to Israel, aged just 18. I'd have never imagined that decades later I'd be riding through the landscape beneath!

I'd originally intended to follow the Israeli National Trail which ran from the northern border to Eilat, and was carrying the guidebook. So when I saw the Trail's red, white and blue markers, I followed them up a steep hillside. I regretted this decision, as the path quickly petered out amid boulders and long dried grass. We were all puffing and sweating heavily as we struggled over and around the rocks on this steep hillside. My enthusiasm waned further when I came to yet another barbed wire fence. A palomino horse and rider passed by and I lifted my head from the fence to greet them – giving a double take when I saw the rider had no shoes! I was still engrossed in unpicking the fence when he returned.

"Where are you going?" he asked,

"Ein Dor," I replied.

"I'll ride with you for a while," he replied, introducing himself as Gabriel. "I rode by quickly before, as I thought you had a stallion." Together we zig-zagged up to the top of the mountain, overlooking Lake Kinneret.

"Cross the gully in the plain over there, and you'll get to Ein Dor," he told me, pointing over the wide expanse of ploughed farmland. I was disappointed it was still so hazy, sensing that if it was clear, the views would be spectacular. As we travelled westwards I kept dismounting to alter Sussita's packs, which were unbalanced and kept shifting to one side – it was one of those days!

Down on the dry brown undulating plains, we passed ploughed land, cattle and cacti. In turn, we were passed by convoys of noisy four wheelers, leaving us in a dust cloud – I was very grateful for my borrowed sunglasses. For a short stretch, I noticed we were back on the Israeli Trail, and here I came across a gaunt young man resting on his pack. He told me he was from the Czech Republic and was aiming for the monastery at the top of Mount Tabor. He had a long way to go before dark, which wasn't far away, so I waved him goodbye and kept following the valley westwards to Kibbutz Ein Dor.

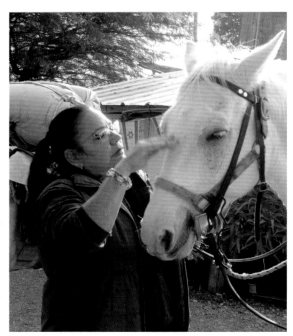

Galit Juli applying fly cream to Zorg.
Below: I asked for water for the horses at a quarry
where Jews and Arabs were working together.

Ein Dor

Ein Dor is mentioned in the Bible (1 Samuel chapter 28). King Saul had expelled all mediums and spiritualists from the land, but when the great Philistine army came to fight him on the Jezreel plains he was terrified. Knowing that the prophet Samuel had died, he asked God for help, but He didn't answer. So Saul disguised himself, found a medium at Ein Dor, and asked him to conduct a seance to communicate with Samuel. Angry that he had disobeyed God, Samuel foretold Saul's death.

Ben met me at the security gate and I followed him on his scooter to the stables, where he helped me untack. He gave the horses hay and water and showed me where I could take a very welcome shower. His mother Galit arrived later, having just judged a horse jumping competition.

"I judge competitions abroad," she told me. "People think we are permanently at war here. In fact, we all work together. Fifteen Arab children with genetic defects come to my stables for therapy." Galit and her horses also work with Israeli Defence Force soldiers who are suffering from shell shock.

"One man was paralysed on his left side, but we got him on a horse and walked him around the kibbutz," she told me. "The movement of the horse loosened his muscles, so riding gave him a sense of freedom. We also had a child who didn't talk, but began speaking after sitting on a horse. Riding is proven to release endorphins, which send signals to the brain – it's easier to learn when you are riding."

We looked at the map and planned my route across the Jezreel plains. "Make sure you cross the plains before it starts raining," Galit told me. Later I would experience torrential rain and mud, and understand her words of warning!

That night I shared the spacious tack room with her two cats, who controlled the mice and snakes. Before I left the next day, Galit applied anti-fly cream to the horses' faces and gave me Uri Shama's contact number at Kibbutz Hazorea, on the western side of the Jezereel plains. She added: "Beware of the jackals. There's rabies in this area."

You are today where your thoughts have brought you.
You will be tomorrow where your thoughts take you. - James Allen

After photographing Zorg and Sussita I had to run to catch them as they walked into the distance.

7. MOUNT TABOR

THE JEZREEL PLAIN

Even through the haze, from far away, I'd been able to see the cone-shaped Mount Tabor (1,886ft, 575 metres). As I left the Kibbutz Ein Dor, for the first time on my ride the atmosphere had cleared, so I was excited to set up my video camera… only to discover the battery was flat. Instead I used my dust-filled SLR camera, trusting that the horses wouldn't charge off!

Mount Tabor was once used as a beacon, to inform the villages in the north of Jewish Holy days and the beginning of the new month. This distinct landmark has seen many battles through the ages. In 55BC, 30,000 Judeans rebelled against the Roman Proconsul and were defeated in battle here.

At least a thousand years earlier, Deborah, a Jewish prophetess, summoned Barak from his home in Kedesh, and told him that God had commanded him to march 10,000 troops against Sisera, who had 900 iron chariots. Barak said he would go only if Deborah went with him, so she agreed, declaring: "Up! For this is the day in which the Lord has delivered Sisera into your hands. Has not the Lord gone out before you?" So Barak and his troops descended Mount Tabor and defeated Sisera's army (Book of Judges, chapter 4).

At the base of Mount Tabor is an ancient trade route, which has had several names, including 'Way of the Philistines' and 'Via Maris', which means 'way of the sea' (recorded in Isaiah 9:1). This linked Egypt to the empires of Syria, Asia Minor and Mesopotamia (now Iraq, Kuwait, Syria and Turkey), and was crossed by other trading routes from Africa to Europe and from Asia to Africa.

Mount Tabor is also thought to be the place of the transfiguration. "Jesus took Peter, James and John up a high mountain and He was transfigured before them. His face shone like the sun, and His clothes became as white as the light, and behold Moses and Elijah appeared to them, talking."

The Jezreel plain was like an enormous, irregular checker board, with patches of crops and brown soil, ploughed in different directions. Dotted over the huge expanse, I spotted some tractors, speedily harrowing before the rain arrived. It felt strange to see huge cities, crammed with tower blocks, edging the vast expanse to the south and towering above the plains to the north.

As I rode through history, with vultures circling overhead, I could sense the fierce battles that had taken place, and imagined the final battle of Armageddon, which Revelations (16 v14,16) tells us will be fought here. "For they are spirits of demons, performing signs, which go out of the whole world, to gather them to the battle of the that great day of God Almighty... and they gathered them together in the place in Hebrew, Armageddon."

We reached the first major road intersection to find barriers standing in our way, so I backtracked to a break in the hedge. Keeping up our momentum, we quickly crossed over between the trucks, and continued west, criss-crossing to avoid trampling the newly sown seed. We arrived at another main road – this time with a concrete barrier in the middle. I found a tunnel underneath, and the horses nervously passed through as traffic echoed overhead.

Crossing a railway bridge, I hailed a driver in a pick-up and asked the way to the Hazorea Kibbutz. At first he didn't understand me and said it was a long way to the coast! I tried again, and this time he told me it wasn't far. Unfortunately it took me off my map, and I didn't have another to cover this new area.

"You will see us riding towards you," Uri told me on the phone, but I could see no sign of them. I asked another driver, who pointed westwards. I urged the horses into a trot, as the sun was sinking fast and so was the battery on my phone. Then it got dark. "Ride toward the hills and the main road to the west, but don't cross it," said Uri. "When you get there, turn right, keep on the track and we will meet you."

I pushed on towards the outline of some olive trees, and trotted between the rows, ducking the low branches, until we reached the busy road. As we turned right, a car pulled up beside me and a young Arab man said, "the horsemen are waiting for you a kilometre down the track."

The headlights of the passing vehicles flashed through gaps in the trees and illuminated our steps. Suddenly Zorg sensed something up ahead and stopped abruptly.

I held his reins tightly. Zorg was frozen to the spot as we saw five horses and riders appear out of the darkness.

"It's all part of the game," said Dani, one of the riders, as I apologised for getting lost. They escorted us under another busy road, past big fishponds, and up through the kibbutz to the stables, with far-reaching views across the Jezreel plain. Uri and his friends helped me unpack the horses, before watering and stabling them, with a good helping of hay and grain. He offered me a whole sack of grain to take on my journey – I was very grateful, but it would have been too heavy, so I took enough for the next few days.

My late arrival had delayed a birthday party for one of their group. I joined them, and learnt that Uri had built the stables and trained horses on the kibbutz. His friends came and rode with him several times a week and once a year they would usually do a longer ride elsewhere in Israel. They came from as far afield as Syria, the Czech Republic and Poland. "Most immigrants came to Israel as children," said Uri. "Those from the west came after the war."

I asked him about the crops I'd seen on the Jezreel plains. "Almond trees and cotton grow well in Israel because they do well on waste water, which has gone through various stages of purification." I'd become familiar with the bright purple pipes, across the countryside, with signs in Hebrew, Arabic and English warning you not to drink the water. Uri said the plains were also used to grow sunflowers, mandarins and olives, and the large fishponds contained ornamental fish, which were exported as far as South America. There was more agriculture and even a plastic factory, here at the kibbutz.

Uri introduced me to his large young mule, called Aviv (Spring) and told me how a group of them had brought an American mule trainer over to Israel.

"A mule is very good for packing out. They are very safe, less energetic, tougher and more surefooted than horses. They also live longer, maybe 35 to 40 years," he explained, "but you need to approach them differently."

"The rain is coming, so take this," he added, handing me a large yellow raincoat, whose hem trailed on the ground. I had been given one just like this in Texas on my ride across America. They must only come in one size as this one was just as big!

Kibbutz Hazorea

Uri gave me his map, indicating where I could cross the roads. He then led me across the kibbutz and made sure I was on the right track. It started off simply enough, but soon I was faced with ploughed fields, and found myself searching for gaps in the hedges and fences.

"You can't ride over here," said one of two men man, standing by a pick-up, brewing coffee, "we've just sown it."

"I'll ride around the edge," I replied. "I'm heading up the valley."

"Okay. Would you like a coffee?"

One of the men, called Nir, gave me his phone number and invited me to stay with him and his wife near Caesarea. He added: "Not quite sure what we will do with the horses though!"

After drinking some strong black coffee, I skirted the field and followed the wadi (Hebrew for valley) to Ramot Menashe, passing some signs which seemed to suggest this was the site of a famous battle. After a few detours, I arrived at Dubi's ranch where several young people helped me unpack the horses.

I could hear music. "It sounds like a party!" I remarked.

"It is!" they replied. "Go inside. We will look after your horses."

It took my eyes a moment to adjust to the dimly lit barn, packed with people watching a band playing Western cowboy songs. Behind them was a large screen showing a film of trick riders performing gymnastics on galloping horses. One of them looked very like the singer on the stage. I soon entered into the swing and clapped along with the rest of the jovial audience.

At the end, I introduced myself to band members Dubi and Ruthie, and told them how much I had enjoyed their performance.

"We like to see people enjoying themselves!" Ruthie beamed. "We take them back to simple joy. They relax and enjoy the atmosphere and one another." Ruthie introduced me to Gili Liber, a famous Israeli musician who had been playing the pipes and singing.

Dubi's Ranch

"We're the kind of people who don't like to be boring!" Dubi told me, and I heard more about their colourful, adventurous life. Ruthie then pointed to an extensive buffet of colourful food, spread over several tables, and invited me to help myself. "Now is the time to eat!" For the next three hours I attempted to finish my plateful, but so many came by to say hello – Druze, Arabs and Jews. I didn't want to miss meeting such interesting people.

"See? We are all friends!" Ruthie smiled. "We all share one piece of land. It's important to get along."

Ihab, a Druze tourist guide, who I had met before and who helped me get to the re-enactment of the ANZAC battle, came over to speak to me. As we were talking, he remarked, "It's all Abraham and Sarah's fault!"

I knew what he meant. Abraham originally came from Ur (probably in modern day Iraq). God told him to leave his country and family (Genesis 12). In faith, Abraham travelled 1,500 miles up the Euphrates to Haran and then south into Canaan (modern day Israel) in about 2100 BC. Although God had promised Abraham and Sarah a son, the years passed by, and when Sarah was past the age of child bearing she gave her Egyptian maid Hagar to Abraham. She had a son called Ishmael, and Abraham assumed this to be the promised son, but God said, "your wife Sarah will bear you a son, and you will call him Isaac. I will establish my covenant with him as an everlasting covenant for his descendants after him." (Genesis 17:19)

When Abraham was over 99 years old, God gave them a miracle son, Isaac, promised to make his nation great and told Abraham, "I will bless those who bless you and curse those who curse you, and in you shall all the nations of the earth be blessed." (Genesis 12v1-3). Jesus Christ was Jewish of course, and a descendant of Abraham. Because he, God's son, made the ultimate sacrifice, those who believe in him are Abraham's heirs, according to God's promise. Both the Arab and Jewish nations are regarded as descendants of Abraham – the Arabs from Ishmael, and the Jews from Isaac.

"I'll shoe your horses, for free!" said Dorron the farrier, with his mohican haircut.

"Why don't you stay longer, have a rest, and we can tell me more about Israel!" added Ruthie.

"We are a group of people who don't want to be boring!"
- Dubi Selmen

I expected to be sleeping in the straw on the barn floor, but Dubi offered me his daughter's empty room in a complex, near the ranch. Ruthie took me there and then took my dirty clothes to wash. I appreciated having my own space and shelter, as the long awaited rain deluged for several days.

The ranch looked like a stage set right out of the Wild West, both inside and out. An old stagecoach and chariot were displayed at the ranch entrance and, around the back, a faded mural of an old Western town acted as a backdrop to the horse corrals. Inside the atmospheric log barn was a rustic bar and around the walls hung old sepia photographs of North American Indians and paintings of cowboys and horses. Down the steps there was a large poster of John Wayne and some famous racehorse posters from films featuring Sea Biscuit and Phar Lap.

Dubi's remark, "We are a group of people who don't want to be boring", was certainly true. I found out more of their adventurous lives, including trick riding, knights in armour, jousting and tentpegging. People now came to their ranch from all over the world to ride through the beautiful countryside.

"You should come back again in March, the flowers here are amazing!" Ruthie enthused, adding, "we have a lot of spring water in this area. As Israel is so small you will find the scenery changes rapidly." They advised me not to go near the Green Line, as the people were very poor.

I remarked that I had met some good horse people already.

"We may not all agree, but Israeli horse people have a good heart!"

Dubi's Ranch - a stage set for the Wild West.

The passion comes from what you don't have
- Dubi Selmen

"I was a city boy in Tel Aviv," Dubi told me. "My father and I were always planning, and dreamt of having a ranch. Passion comes from what you don't have."

He continued: "The British were good to start with, but during the British Mandate my father was in a resistance group and was jailed for six years. Some of his group were hanged. I was six years old when I asked my father whether he went too far. Isn't life the most important thing? My father replied, "No, liberty is the most important"."

"In 1948, when he was 27 years old, Dubi's father-in-law sailed a ship carrying 5,000 Jewish holocaust survivors from Europe," Ruthie told me. "It was rammed by a British ship, and sent back to Europe, but this helped persuade the United Nations to consent to an independent Jewish nation."

Dubi could remember the Six Day War in 1967. "I was 11 years old when seven states around us, Egypt, Jordan, Syria, Lebanon, Morocco, Libya and Iraq, declared they were going to push us into the sea. Fearing for our lives, we slept in a bomb shelter, but awoke to see newspapers full of stories of victory. They told us that our airforce had destroyed theirs in a single day."

Dubi started to learn both music and riding when he was seven, and was taught to ride by British and Russian police. "My teacher was a commander in the Russian army."

Ruthie and Dubi told so many interesting stories. Ruthie was also from the city. Her family could be traced back to the Spanish inquisition in the 15th to 16th centuries, when the Jews were expelled from Spain. Muslims and Protestants also became targets of this Inquisition.

Ruthie continued: "When I first went to America, I worked my way across the country. I was a cowgirl on a ranch in Nebraska with real, tough cowboys, living just as they did 100 years earlier."

She then went on to California and learnt trick riding. "I was nicknamed the flying Jew!" she laughed. "Trick riding requires a combination of speed, technique and courage. You have to let go of the reins and gallop at full speed!" She said the men rely on their strength, but the women develop better technique.

"In trick riding you have to feel exactly where the horse's legs are all the time. It's all about creating a bond, a special connection," explained Ruthie. "When you decide to go, there is no turning back. You have to go! Everything happens very fast. It is incredibly athletic and daring." Both she and Dubi worked as stunt riders, and Ruthie played the part of Annie Oakley in California.

        "I wanted to pioneer these skills in Israel, so I bought horses at an auction in California, trained them and flew them back to Israel. We performed here for ten years and were the only trick riders in Israel," she added. "I taught my skills to students, who called me Mum! Trick riding combined all my talents – I had found my destiny!"

        She and Dubi have been in partnership for 30 years. "He is an exceptional horseman, who can train any horse. If one has problems, he will melt its heart and make it believe again."

        People bring him horses from all over the country, and he has trained horses for television, film and even for opera, including a performance of Carmen, which had 12 horses on stage. "When they were filming Masada, he had to wear a skirt (Roman costume) for three months!"

        "He has trained a sheep. Even a pig!" Ruthie exclaimed.

        "I told you I hate to be boring!" Dubi confirmed.

Dani Gold

Dani Gold came to escort me back to his home in Binyamina, and my horses had to jog to keep pace with his quick-stepping Tennessee Walker Humi (which means brownie). "A Tennessee Walker travels at 7 to 8 kilometres an hour (up to 5mph)," Dani stated as we followed the dry Crocodile River.

"There are two thoughts as to why this river got its name," he told me, "either because there were crocodiles living in the river, or more likely because roman gladiators wrestled with crocodiles in the stadium at Binyamina."

En route Dani showed me several underground aqueducts, which transported water through tunnels all the away to Caesarea. "They had great ingenuity!" he said, pointing to a dam which helped to collect the water.

Dani had spent a few years diving for tropical fish in the Red Sea on the Sinai Peninsula, which they exported to Europe. He had also worked as a security guard on El Al flights and as a beekeeper.

"My wife Vivi and I kept bees for 12 years. Our kids used to help too – they got stung many times! When we collected the honey, we had to drive it quickly into the garage and shut the doors as other bees would follow us in and steal it." They had 150 hives, each of which produced 40kg (88lb) of honey. In the spring they would place them in the citrus groves and, later in the year, they moved them to Galilee. This meant the honey had different flavours, including citrus, clover and eucalyptus.

"As a family, we bottled it and people would come and buy it – especially at Rosh Hashanah in September, the Jewish New Year, when it's traditional to eat honey with apple, in the hope that the next year will be sweet 'in the land of milk and honey'!"

Dani continued: "I sold my beekeeping business just in time, as the quantity and price of honey dropped, and went straight into the pizza business. Israelis love pizzas! It was very hard work and a big challenge, but I went for it and bought 21 pizza places. Now we have 62!"

He went on to talk about his passion for riding horses. "I used to dream of riding horses, but my first ride was on a donkey, which was owned by a shepherd who was passing by with 100 sheep. "Will you let me ride your donkey?" I asked. "Bring me cold water," the shepherd replied. I did, and in return he let me have five minutes on the donkey. Then he asked for another glass of water and I got another five minutes!

"I started to ride properly when I was 30, and now I get to ride around the country for a month every year with friends." Hearing this, I understood why Rauven had been so keen for me to contact Dani.

We stopped for a snack at his grand new barn, which was under construction at Amikam, and then rode on to his home in the settlement of Binyamina – named after Binyamina Rothschild who donated money to buy the land. I met Vivi (short for Reviva, meaning morning dew) and enjoyed their relaxed hospitality for several days.

I was very blessed to have 'fallen in' with the hospitable Israeli horse people once again. At Dani and Vivi's home, I met their sons and families over the Shabbat meal, and the following day, Dani guided me through the vineyards to visit the ancient theatre at Jabotinsky Park, where the Romans once wrestled crocodiles. In 1914, Baron Edmond de Rothschild set up an agriculture school for Jewish farmers here, and they later established the nearby agricultural settlements of Binyamina and Giva'at Ada – now world-class vineyards.

It was a complex route and I doubted I would have ever reached the Mediterranean on my own. Dani led us along tracks, across ploughed fields and through banana plantations, where there were many Thai workers. I asked Dani about this.

"During the intifada in 1997, when tensions were high between Arabs and Jewish workers, there were many stabbings. When it happened again in 2000, we realised this could not go on, so instead we hired Thai people. They are peaceful, work well in agriculture and in restaurants and earn good wages to send home. When they return to Thailand after five years, they are considered wealthy."

A locked barricade barred our route, but Dani, riding Humi, beckoned me to follow along the steep-sided edge of a dry river until we got to the main road. Here, I kept Zorg trotting immediately behind Humi, so he wouldn't shy at the rubbish on the road.

"Nearly all of this village's 14,000 inhabitants come from one of two African families," Dani remarked, "and most of them have married, so there are genetic problems as well as crime and drug problems. There is no room to build more houses, so they build upwards, adding more floors as their children grow up and have children of their own."

We edged the town on the western side, where the rubbish was piled high and there was a strong stench of sewage. We came to a flat wooden bridge, but Zorg didn't want to cross, so I dismounted to lead them. Sussita walked across calmly, but Zorg took a leap, knocking me into the mud and landing in the water. He then struggled and got his front knees on the bridge, stuck half in and half out. As I held his head, Dani quickly checked to see if his legs were caught, and once we knew they weren't, we encouraged him to scramble out.

"There must be the Arab blood in him to do something like that!" Dani remarked. "He seems OK." I was very relieved that he only had a few scratches and didn't smell of sewage.

Jaser Al Zarka

Beyond the northern end of the beach, where a handful of fisherman eke out
a living, is a nature reserve containing old Roman ruins. To the south lies
Caesarea, a Jewish resort town where Prime Minister Benjamin Netanyahu
has a home. It seemed strange that the poorest and the richest lived next to
each other on the same stretch of coast, and the contrast was very apparent.
One moment we were riding past rubble, and the next we were clip-clopping
along neat pavements, weaving between shapely trees and watered,
manicured grass verges. Although out of sight from their Arab neighbours,
there was no escaping the Muslim call to prayer, broadcast from speakers
five times a day.

The Turkish bridge was built in 1898 for the visit of the German Kaiser Wilhelm II to Palestine

8. THE MEDITERRANEAN SEA

I was excited when we eventually reached the Mediterranean and rode across the sand. I've always loved riding horses on the beach, and have many good memories of speeding along empty beaches when I rode the length of New Zealand many years previously.

    We passed an area where sea water was evaporated to create salt, and then carried along the ancient route of the Via Maris (the way of the sea), which ran from Egypt to the modern day countries of Iran, Iraq, Turkey and Syria. "Inland, it was all swamps until the beginning of the last century," Dani informed me.

Dani was an informative riding companion, and was very good at leading my horses. I also really appreciated not having to bury my head in a map at every turn.

On the northern side of the coast, where a few fishing boats were anchored, we tied our horses to some signs and ate nuts and tangerines. Both Zorg and Sussita pulled back, but surprisingly nothing broke this time.

Caesarea

We followed an ancient aqueduct – originally built by Herod (37BC to 4BC) and dedicated to Caesar Augustus. Water was brought from the south side of Mount Carmel along a single raised canal, all the way to the old city of Caesarea. In order for the water to flow by gravity, the aqueduct was built on arches with a carefully measured gradient. When they needed more water, the Legions of Emperor Hadrian (2AD) built a second aqueduct, doubling its width and bringing water from the Crocodile River (where we had ridden the day before) through a three and a half mile tunnel (6 kilometres). The aqueduct carried water for 1,200 years, fed by additional channels built by the Crusaders.

Nearing the end of the old aquaduct, a man hailed Dani, saying his son was celebrating his Bar Mitzvah, and asking if he could have a ride on his horse. Bar Mitzvah is a coming-of-age celebration for 13-year-old boys. Girls celebrate the Mitzvah, usually at 12. As the boy clambered onto Humi, Dani led him along across the sand.

The Romans also developed the harbour at the old city of Caesarea, using special lime mortar which sets under water. Their 40 acre (16 hectare) harbour could accommodate 300 ships. The ruins of the city were excavated in the fifties and sixties, and became a national park in 2011.

9. THE GREEN LINE

"Believe me, you didn't miss a thing by not riding to the Green Line, West Bank and Tel Aviv!" Dani assured me as he and Vivi transported me and my horses south, through the middle of the country. The Green Line was named after the green ink used to draw a line on the map, while the armistice talks were going on in 1949. This lay to the east, with busy main roads and the urbanised sprawl of Tel Aviv to the west, so we had avoided dangers on both sides.

"It's a small country, and everyone wants to live in the centre," Dani said. Vivi added: "Building here these days is very expensive, as you also need a bomb shelter with air filters in case of chemical attack."

She continued: "This is the narrowest part of the country – there's just a 12 kilometre (7.5 mile) passage between Netanya and the West Bank wall. The Green line is actually a squiggle!" Dani pointed out the Green Line wall, and told me it was built to prevent snipers from shooting at passing vehicles.

Israel, Dani insisted, provides equal rights to everyone, Arab or Jew, man or woman. "A lot of Arabs are very happy to live here, as we have democracy and our economy is good – especially when they see how neighbouring countries are struggling." More than 500 million Muslims live in this region, compared with just seven million Jews.

Passing through one neighbourhood, Vivi remarked, "you could sleep on the road here on a Saturday. This is an Ultra Orthodox neighbourhood, and absolutely no one will drive on Shabbatt."

We stopped to visit a smallholding owned by Eyal and Tal Bartov – an endurance horseman and photographer. He showed me some of his beautiful footage of wildlife in Israel. He also checked out my camera, confirmed there was dust in the lens, and remarked, "it's an old camera!"

"It's only six years old!" I replied. "They suffer from being slung over the front of my saddle, so I didn't bring my newest camera." My lenses also dislike being continually jostled about on horseback – I had to buy a new one after my ride across Southern Europe. I knew that most people like to have 'state of the art' technology, but I tend to hang on to equipment so long as it works okay. People always laugh at me when I tell them my laptop is fairly new, and they discover it's ten years old!

Despite being such a small country, Israel is a world leader in technology. Since independence in 1948, the Israelis have invented drip irrigation, the cherry tomato, the electric car grid and the USB memory stick to name just a few. Eyal showed me his mirrorless camera, which did tempt me, as it was so much lighter than my SLR. He told me it was good enough to film documentaries.

Tal Shahar

We drove through the security gate at Shepherd's Spring Farm, south of Tel Aviv, and were greeted by a pack of white dogs and Moshe Franko, leading a pretty grey horse, closely followed by her new black colt.

Moshe breeds Missouri Fox Trotter horses. Like Dani's Tennessee Walkers, they are comfortable to ride and cover the ground quickly, if with a slight different gait. They had ridden across Israel many times, and there was friendly banter about which was the best breed. Moshe showed us the horses and his Simmental Ballard cattle – a local breed which he fed on cotton straw – as we toured the stables, yards and tack rooms, made from converted railway carriages. On a rise above us stood the large house.

"My wife and I started with two carriages and kept building as our family increased," he explained. Inside, the kitchen was furnished with beautiful rustic wood furniture made by his wife Sharon, who was at the time leading a Jeep tour of Africa.

Moshe and Dani examined Hebrew maps and advised me of the best route to Beersheba (Beersheva), and from there to Moshe's friend Ilan, on the edge of the Ramon Crater. Later Moshe showed me the route I was to follow in the morning, between plantations of avocado trees and jojoba plants. I took mental photographs as we travelled towards an impressive sunset.

The cockerels woke me early and I was packed up when Moshe brought me a fresh bread stick, and fruit, which I squashed into my saddle bags.

"Call me if you have any problems, right?" he said. "I'm in charge until you get to Ilan at the Ramon Crater."

"You Israeli horse people are amazing!' I said gratefully. I urged the horses into a trot, pushing on hard to cover the 22 miles (35km) to my next stop.

Harvest Time

I followed the track which ran parallel to the railway, and then crossed over a bridge, turning south across a dry, undulating landscape chequered with plantations and olive groves. Some men were extracting honey from beehives, and the bees were swarming angrily, so I kept my distance and carried on. I was puzzled to hear an intermittent, mechanical vibrating sound, and tied the horses to an olive tree and went to investigate. I found a tractor driving from one tree to another, where a machine would clutch the trunk and shake it violently, so that most of its olives fell into nets beneath. Others were knocked out of the branches by men wielding long sticks. I met a tall, friendly foreman and asked if I could take photos. He told me the harvesters came from Hebron in the West Bank, and had been doing this for generations. They liked to work in Israel because it was better paid.

Gathering the nets full of olives.   The friendly foreman who chatted to me about the olive harvest.

"Most of the olives are used for oil," the foreman told me, and explained that the harvest starts after the first rain and goes on to Hanukkah (also known as Chanukah) in late November or December. This Jewish holiday commemorates the rededication of the Holy Temple in Jerusalem at the time of the Maccabean (Maccabim) Revolt (167 to 160 BC) against the Greek Empire. It is also known as the Festival of Lights and the Feast of Dedication, and is observed by lighting the candles in the nine-branched candelabrum called a Hanukkah Menorah. One candle is lit each night, ending on the final night of the festival.

As I passed a huge power station, I paused to take photos because the light was beautiful, but I didn't linger – hearing rumbles of thunder and seeing rain clouds approaching from the east. I had been warned that when it rained in Israel, it really rained!

The first raindrops fell as I skirted around a hill which features in the story of Samson (Shimshon) (Judges 13-16). He was a Nazarite, which meant he couldn't eat or drink anything from the grape, go near a dead body, or cut his hair. God anointed Samson with supernatural strength and he ruled Israel for 20 years. But his downfall came when his Philistine mistress discovered that his strength came from his hair. While he was sleeping, she shaved his head and he awoke to find the strength and presence of the Lord had left him (Judges 16:20). The Philistines captured him and gouged out his eyes, and while they were making a public spectacle of him, he cried out to God, who again granted him supernatural strength. Samson pushed against the columns of a building, brought it crashing down, and he and his persecutors were killed.

I quickly pulled on Uri's large yellow raincoat, which so vast that when sitting in the saddle it was like a tent, covering all my saddle bags. The sprinkle soon became a deluge, and neither Zorg nor Sussita wanted to move another step. Hopeful that it might be a passing shower, we sheltered by some small trees, but the rain only got stronger. So I urged the horses on towards a stream, where I dismounted, and led them over to drink, but they refused to step down the slope. I tripped over my long coat and landed in the heavy clay. All of us were soon caked in mud, as we slipped and slithered around the stream.

Omri Canaan

Kibbutz Nir and Ajur Moshav

Rosie Canaan

Jechezkel Rotanberg

Pressing olive oil.

Finally I reached Kibbutz Nir, and made it through the security gates by closely following a car. We headed for a big barn, but both horses refused to go into the dark shelter, despite my best efforts to persuade them. I was getting more and more frustrated, as my saddle bags, camera bag, pack, bed roll got more and more soaked. While pulling the horses with one hand, I fumbled for my phone with the other, trying to find the number for my contact at the kibbutz… only for my phone to slip out of my hand and crash onto the concrete floor. Amazingly it still worked, and I managed to contact Bor, who told me to make my way to the cattle yards. Here, two young men helped me unpack the horses and we piled the sodden tack into their tack room, which was a large shipping container. As the horses tucked into their straw, a car pulled up.

"You are staying with us tonight on the Ajur Moshav!" stated a wiry man, introducing himself as Omri.

"Okay, thank you!" I replied, with no idea where we were going. As I undid my bootlaces on his doorstep, Omri introduced me to his wife Rosie, who surprised me with a perfect English accent. He and her eldest daughter Alma made me a pot of tea. "You seem very English!" I observed.

"I am English!" Rosie replied. "When I was seven, my parents decided to leave our comfortable home in Greenwich, London, to start a more meaningful life in the Jewish State. They made 'Aliya' in 1987 and we settled in Jerusalem."

Rosie put a plateful of food in front of me and while I ate it, I met her youngest daughter Ruth and her son Noah, returning from basketball practice. As we chatted I asked her about life in the moshav (settlement). "I've been a costume designer for the last 14 years and have worked with dance companies like Vertigo, based in the Ella Valley, who have performed at the Albert Hall and many theatres."

Omri told me he was a welder and fencer, as well as a keen endurance rider, who kept several Arab horses in his barn. He advised me against riding past the Dead Sea during my journey back north to Jerusalem as it was "remote, rough and only inhabited by Bedouin". They seated me in a comfortable chair in front of their big wood burning stove, and I only moved from there to have a shower.

"If you want to ride up to Jerusalem from this side, I can ride with you!" he offered.

The following morning Rosie returned me to Kibbutz Nir, where my horses had been overnighting. She introduced me to Jechezkel Rotanberg, who showed me how olives were processed and gave me a bottle of freshly pressed olive oil, which I placed in my saddle bags – already weighed down with fresh fruit from Bor, who then took me on a quick tour of the cattle yards in his Gater.

"The cows eat a mixture of chicken poo and citrus fruit which ferments for at least 30 days," he informed me. "But not the beef cattle. They have barley combined with olive leaves and cotton stalks." He offered to take my laundry and said he would deliver it to me at my next stop. Once I had saddled up, he directed me to his friend Liad Cohen at Beit Guvrin-Maresha National Park, along an empty road that was still being built.

I met Liad at a junction and followed him in his pick-up to the entrance of Beit Guvrin-Maresha, a World Heritage Site, and located at an important junction between Egypt, Hebron and Jerusalem. I tied my horses to some trees near the entrance and jumped into Liad's pick-up. He took me on a whistle stop tour of the park's attractions, including interesting caves, which have had many uses over the years – including quarries, dovecotes, tombs, olive presses, baths, hiding places, storage chambers and shelters for farm animals. Caves such as these are commonplace in the Judean lowlands, because the rocks consist of soft, light-coloured chalk that is easy to quarry and are often covered with a harder crust.

An information leaflet told me that the Israel Nature and Parks Authority manages more than 150 nature reserves, often in archaeological sites, and protecting 2,500 species of indigenous wild plants, 20 species of fish, 400 species of birds and 70 species of mammals. In the Bible, Maresha is mentioned as one of the cities built by Rehoboam (2 Chronicles 11: 5-8), and there's also the remains of a large Byzantine church, named after Mary, the mother of Jesus.

"Our wildlife is very fragile," said Liad. "Israel is very crowded, and with the wall separating the West Bank, the animals can't get across – the only things that can get past the wall are the honey badgers and birds." He continued: "We have eagle eyed owls and wildcats. There used to be 100 caracal (large cats) in Israel but they have died out when their habitat and food disappeared."

Beit Guvrin-Maresha National Park

I noticed his pistol, which was casually sticking out of the waistband of his jeans.

"It's to stop poaching," he told me. I could sense his dedication and passion as he talked about the wildlife. "It's a 24-hour, day-to-day fight to keep our wildlife."

The walls of the caves were decorated with paintings, and the Bell Cave was especially spectacular – it was hewn between the Byzantine and Early Muslim period and is now home to seven different species of bats. Another cave had over 2,000 well preserved niches, carved out for doves to nest in. They have been found in 85 similar caves, so we know that doves were once popular all over the Judean lowlands. They were bred for their meat and eggs, for sacrificial rituals, and their droppings were used as fertiliser.

The hospitable female attendant in the entrance booth gave me a cup of coffee from her own flask and some chocolate. "In Israel, you'll find the military everywhere," said Liad, pointing out the military zones on my map, and directing me on to Lachish my next stop.

I found myself near an army base and could see them firing, so I tried to take a detour, but I came across a military gate at every turn. After several dead ends I got back on track, but by now the sun was sinking and I was again racing against time. Trotting past row upon row of vines, I managed to overshoot the turning into Lachish in the dark, and with my phone battery dying, I plugged it into the battery charger and looked at maps on the screen. It suggested there were 17km to go, but I was convinced I was in the right area. Feeling tired and frustrated, I called Dan Harkabi and told him I would camp right where I was, as there was grass and trees to tie the horses.

"Do you see a light?" said Dan. "That's me. Come towards the light!" Eventually I found him in the gloom of the vineyard and thanked him for coming to meet us.

"We had no choice," he said jovially. "We'd only just landed from the US when Moshe and Ilan called me! We're good friends, so we had to obey their command!"

We leisurely retraced our previously hurried steps past the ghostly shadows of the vines. Dan led Sussita and light heartedly chatted about the time when the Israelite spies, including Joshua and Caleb, came to check out the promised land and returned with huge grapes, to show Moses and the Israelites.

As we arrived at Lachish settlement, I could hear a pack of guard dogs and understood why they didn't need a gate. Yael, Dan's wife, told me they were Canaan dogs, a breed which has been here for thousands of years – used by the ancient Israelites to guard their flocks and camps. When the Israelites were forcibly removed from their land, it is thought they left their dogs behind, who reverted to the wild. They remain undomesticated today, and having ridden past them many times and been barked at loudly, I could confirm that they were excellent guard dogs!

10. Lachish

"If you want to make a difference, you can't be like everyone else." – Dan Harkari

"Arab horses make life fun!" Dan remarked as he led Sussita into a yard beside a barn full of this beautiful breed. "These are Shagiya Arabs from Europe. We use them for endurance riding, where you cover 100 miles (160km) in 12 hours. My son and I have represented Israel for the past two years."

Once the horses had water and hay, we headed for a unique wooden house, which he and his wife Hael had designed and imported from Finland, along with a team of builders who assembled it in ten days. Dan showed me the prototype for his latest invention, on the kitchen table.

"While my wife was pregnant, I have also been pregnant with my idea!" he said. "She is a dentist, and we have been both working on this 'Smart Mirror' for the past two years." Yael demonstrated by putting the mirror in her own mouth, and a camera projected the image onto a screen. "I have nine patents in America to cover many aspects of my inventions," he added. "If you want to make a difference, you can't be like everyone else."

He had also developed the USB flash drive and also served in the Israeli airforce for over 20 years. We drank their homegrown wine and ate delicous dates, while Dan cooked supper and talked about his inventions. I was heading for bed when I asked if it would be safe to go out and feed my horses early in the morning – conscious that the guard dogs were loose outside.

"Don't go out, no!" Yael warned me. "We have no boundary fence. When another dog wandered onto our land… it was not good." I headed off to bed trying not to dwell on the dog's plight. It was quite strange to find myself locked in, when I had got used to being locked out!

Dan escorted me to the ancient ruins of Lachish.

"What a laundry service!" Dan exclaimed early the next day, when Bor's friend Mati delivered my clean washing. He also brought half a bucket of whole maize for the horses, which was so thoughtful, although their digestion wasn't used to it, so I didn't risk feeding it to them.

Dan escorted me on horseback to the ruins of the ancient city of Lachish. Archaeologists have found layer upon layer of brutal history, including a ramp built by the conquering Assyrians to reach the outer wall, so that their soldiers could storm the city. This fierce battle was confirmed by hundreds of arrowheads found on the ramp and around the city walls, and 1,500 skulls discovered in a cave nearby.

The Bible's Book of Joshua refers to Lachish in chapter 10 (verses 3, 5, 23, 31-35), and tells us about the Israelites, led by Joshua, and the conquest of Canaan (around 1400 BC). Japhia, the king of Lachish, was one of the five Amorite kings, including the kings of Jerusalem and Hebron, who fought to repel the Israelite invasion. But God was with Joshua, who marched all night with his army and took the city. As the Amorites fled, God sent large hailstones from heaven which killed as many as the Israelites had killed with the sword.

"You must go to the British Museum. They have a whole room devoted to Lachish," added Dan.

As we rode through a vineyard, he asked a Thai worker to cut me a bunch of grapes. "These are like the grapes that Joshua and Caleb took back to show Moses and the people!"

I thanked the worker and carefully laid them in my saddle bag, wondering how soon they would get squashed, but incredibly they survived until I had eaten the very last one! Dan left me on the right track and said goodbye.

"I hope it was worth coming to see us last night?" he asked.

"Absolutely!" I replied shaking his hand. "It's been really interesting. Thank you and God bless you!"

"And you too," he replied, "but don't make Him work too hard!" I chuckled and as I rode away. I was glad nothing was too much for my God!

The chariots of God are tens of thousands, thousands upon thousands. Psalm 68:18

We abruptly emerged from the vineyards and into open, rolling plains. For a while, we followed the Israel National Trail, where I met a Swiss couple who had been cycling around the world for the past five years!

"Keep the railway line on your right and head east of the big power station," Mati had said, so I did as I was told, passing between cultivated land to one side and military land on the other. With each mile travelled south, the landscape became increasingly barren, with only small desert trees surviving in the dry wadis (ravines). I was taking photos of this contrasting landscape when suddenly a white four-by-four vehicle sped towards me, blasting its horn. The driver jammed on the brakes and started yelling at me in Hebrew.

"Sliha Anglis (sorry, English)," I replied and he immediately switched languages.

"What are you doing?" he demanded. "I saw you taking photographs of our helicopters." Another vehicle arrived and an officer, accompanied by a solder holding a gun, approached me and the horses. I told him I was riding horses through Israel and heading for Beersheba.

"Give me your camera," he ordered. Confronted with four tense men, and with two tired horses, a quick getaway across the barren plains was out of the question, so I gingerly did as he asked. My heart sank, knowing that camera contained every photo I had taken on this journey. He told me to flick through the photos, and examined each one closely.

"Okay, go to Beersheba. Don't take pictures," he commanded, tensely. Clutching my camera, and not daring to say a word, I turned the horses south and didn't look back. I didn't even dare to remove my camera from its case until we reached the protection of a wadi.

"The army is everywhere," I remembered someone saying, and they were right. Even when I couldn't see them, I could hear the constant drone of fighter planes above the clouds. Me and my packhorse must have been a suspicious sight – in a world of terrorist attacks and suicide bombings, any large bag could be seen as a threat.

Mati had called ahead to David Hat Shemesh, a sheep farmer based further south. I was looking forward to meeting him, as I had once had my own sheep and was interested in seeing their different breeds. When fierce, barking Canaan dogs barred my progress, I called David, who told me I wasn't far away, so I made a detour around the dogs' territory and followed a track to his farmyard, which was encircled by barns and attractive old railway carriages. In front of one of these David helped me unpack the horses. He slid open the carriage door and I stepped into a cool, dark wooden container, equipped with a kitchen and a bathroom, with solar heated water.

"You can treat this as your hotel," he said, handing me some sheets. "You just have to make your own bed!"

I liked it better than any hotel and relished the idea of staying overnight. It would be fun to live in one of these old wooden train carriages – especially the one over the yard with its wooden decking. Here, I drank tea and played backgammon with David and one of his farmworkers, both of them smoking pipes. I enjoyed this simple game, especially since I won a game (with a little help!).

"Local takeaway!" said David, offering me his mother's homemade macaroni. His parents had moved from New York and California 25 years ago, and his father was now a lawyer in Tel Aviv. David told me he had 400 Dorper ewes, which he informed me came from the Dorset Horn in England. He pointed to his Cyprus goats, with their beautiful big floppy ears: "They give good milk."

I enjoyed staying on the sheep farm, even though I was conscious that this was dangerous territory, seeing the pistols that both David and his employee carried in the back of their jeans. I also noticed that young people from the HaShomer HaChadash organisation, which protects rural farmers, were guarding the farm at night.

Every day, as I rode further south, the landscape was becoming more arid. I was approaching the Negev desert, which covers more than half of Israel, and passed sprawling Bedouin settlements. I felt sorry for a lone grey horse who spotted Zorg and Sussita and whinnied frantically, while doing circuits on his tethering rope. He clearly had no equine friends, only camels.

On my way to the outskirts of Beersheba, where I was to meet Ilan Dvir, Moshe's friend, I met a French girl. She was heading north, and said she had been walking on her own from Paris for the past six months.

The northern city outskirts had expanded beyond the boundary shown on Moshe's old map, so while Ilan was trying to find us in the city, I was actually further north. After several phone calls and frustrated attempts to send him my location, he eventually arrived with a trailer. The horses were happy to have water and to be loaded up and transported through the huge city of Beersheba. From there, we headed south to the Alpaca Farm near the Ramon Crater.

Ilan brought water for the horses and we were all relieved to have a ride in a trailer through metropolis of Beersheba, south to the Alpaca Farm.

"If Moshe says, I obey!" Ilan told me. I realised that Moshe Franko must be a respected and influential man. I offered to pay for his fuel, but he was as generous as his other Israeli horses friends and replied, "we are friends are we not?"

"Moshe and I went to college and then to South America together," Ilan recounted as he drove, "and that's where I had my first meeting with alpacas. I spent two years of my life with them in South America. In 1987 my wife Naama and I went to the Andes and brought a plane full of 180 alpacas and 11 llamas back to Israel.

"The Israeli customs had a problem when we arrived, as we had one more than when we left – a baby was born on the way!" He smiled at the thought, and added: "We have been at the Ramon Crater now for 30 years. Our six children have loved hearing these stories as they have grown up!"

Sharon Keinan mending a fence.

11. THE ALPACA FARM

"The Alpaca Farm is on the Negev highlands, higher than Jerusalem," Ilan explained as he drove through Mitspe Ramon, perched on the edge of the Ramon Crater. Ten minutes later we reached the Alpaca Farm gates.

I was surprised to see so many animals – not just alpacas and llamas, but also horses, sheep, angora goats, donkeys, camels, pigs and poultry. They were kept in large pens, watched by hundreds of pigeons perched on rustic posts and rails. As the horses stepped out of the trailer, their heads were up, ears forward, eyes bright and alert, taking in their new surroundings. I was surprised that Zorg didn't react to the alpacas and llamas – not even when they were fed, and the llamas stretched out their necks through the fencing to steal grain and hay from under their noses!

I met Sharon Keinan, an enthusiastic horsewoman who I'd spoken to while I staying at Dubi's ranch in the north. I was immediately drawn by her warm enthusiasm, and she became a great support for the remainder of my journey in Israel.

Sharon showed me around the farm, which was like a free range zoo. People would come here from all over the world, and stay in the cabins dotted around the perimeter. There was a barn, where the fine alpaca wool was processed and spun, and a visitor centre where beautiful finished products were on sale.

I was excited to be in the Negev desert – such a contrast from the wet, cool climate of Britain. I was given a comfortable little chalet to stay in, and early the following morning I went for a stroll up the glowing brow of a desert hill, accompanied by some collie dogs. I felt energised by the beauty of the cool and glowing desert in the clear early morning light, and walked past vineyards and olive groves, completing a six mile (10km) circuit back to the farm. I returned to find that animal breakfast was being served – they were all waiting attentively at the railings as a wagon, piled high with hay, made its way from one pen to another. It was followed by a trail of free range llamas and alpacas, helping themselves!

Ilan Dvir feeding while (below) some help themselves!

Although alpacas and llamas come from the Chilean Andeas, some 13,000 feet (4,000m) above sea level, where the temperature can be 40 degrees lower than the Negev Highlands, they seem to thrive here. This high desert region has hot days and cold nights, but their wool insulates them from both heat and cold. Alpaca wool can come in 32 different shades and the quality is measured in microns (the thickness of the fibre). The thinner the fibre, the better it traps the air.

   Sharon and her daughter Ronny accompanied me on an evening stroll through the beautiful desert, along with one of the llamas – often used by visitors to carry equipment, picnics and even children on these sunset walks. Surprisingly, Zorg and Sussita didn't seem to mind this rather different looking animal tagging along!

Sharon Keinan and Ilan Dvir above the Alpaca Farm.

Sharon and Ronny her daughter with Mitzpe Ramon in the background.

12. The Negev desert

"We had to make you fall in love with Arabs and the desert!"

The Ramon Crater is only a short distance from the Alpaca Farm, just over a rise in the desert. As I rode up a steep incline, I wasn't prepared for the spectacular scene suddenly laid before me – a breathtaking view of a deep canyon, in many shades of desert colour.

There are five craters in the Negev, including HaMakhtesh HaGadol (big crater), HaMakhtesh HaKatan (small crater) and the Ramon Crater. A makhtesh is a geological formation with steep walls, and a canyon containing a variety of coloured rocks and diverse flora and fauna. They are usually drained by a ravine called a wadi.

I enjoyed staying several days on the Alpaca Farm and had several rides on their Arab horses, which could cover eight and a half miles (14km) every 30 minutes – such a contrast to my packhorses, who would take half a day! Speed simply wasn't possible for a horse carrying a pack, which would thump on their back and could lead to saddle sores, even though I took care to alternate horses.

It wasn't just the speed of the Arab horses which impressed me, it was also the way they could charge over the rocky landscape without stumbling. They never seemed to tire and were always eagerly pulling at the bit, wanting to go even faster. I had to steer my horse away from the one in front, as it flicked up small stones into my face. I was glad I had sunglasses.

"Arabs were bred for speed, the heat and the desert," Sharon remarked. "I used them in the toughest endurance ride in the world, the Teves in America, which covers 100 miles (160km) in 24 hours. There were 230 competitors and only half completed the course – I came 36th." She added: "We have a round-the-crater endurance ride here every November. It's great fun, you should come!"

Desert Nubian Ibex

Sharon was also a good photographer – I was impressed at how she whipped out her phone and took pictures on the move. I did ask myself why I lugged a heavy SLR camera around, especially one that was full of dust, forcing me to focus manually. I thought back to the days when I started out as a photographer, using a manual Olympus OM1, and had to set the light meter and focus every shot. It made me appreciate the advantages of autofocus, especially when travelling with two horses.

We returned to find Ilan leading out an old chestnut horse. "This is my favourite. We got him 30 years ago, with other wild horses from the Golan Heights. He had a perfect metabolism and was great for endurance, as he loved to go fast. We took him to Italy for endurance riding and my son came third!"

Sharon treated me to a delicious 'yoffi' falafel in Mitzpe Ramon, where we saw Nubian ibex males at battle. It was the beginning of the breeding season and they were fighting for the right to mate with the females. Putting their whole body weight behind them, they smacked into each other, causing a loud crack and making me wonder how they didn't have a bad headache.

Sharon was a gifted organiser, made me an appointment for an amazing massage, and helped me to plan the next stage of my journey. I had expected to ride to Eilat in the south of Israel, but decided not to, as it meant crossing a lot of desert and army training areas, and there would be a lack of water and security for the horses at night. Instead, I decided to loop north to Jerusalem via the Dead Sea and Judean desert. Sharon and Ilan planned my route, and called horse contacts to make sure I had safe overnight stops and shelter, as a bad storm was forecast.

After treating me to a tasty omelette, Ilan dropped me, the horses and Sharon on our route to the ancient fortification of Avdat. This small Nabatean settlement stands on the 'incense route' which extended from the Arabian Peninsula to the port of Gaza, and then on to all parts of the Roman Empire. The lucrative incense trade required the construction of waystations, fortresses and towers, offering security, services and supplies to the traders and the camel caravans.

All the goods, including spices, medicinal plants, textiles, dyes, silver and gold were carried by camels. Not only could they survive with little water and high temperatures, but each animal could manage as much as 440lbs (200kg) in weight. The stations were located every 18 miles or so (30km) along the route, which was how much a camel could cover every day.

We rode up to Advat, the old Nabatean station no 62 on the incense route.

Salman the Bedouin

Many Nabateans lived in the Negev and around Petra, and turned to farming when income from the trade routes dried up. They introduced new ways to collect and direct water, built stone terraces to prevent the soil erosion, and produced high quality wine. During the Byzantine period (4th century), Avdat grew into a large village, with cisterns and storerooms to hold produce from agriculture, and workshops to process it, but a huge earthquake destroyed the settlement and it was abandoned.

I enjoyed riding with Sharon, who introduced me to interesting people and places. We visited her Bedouin friend Salman, who was giving a talk about the fast-disappearing traditions of this ancient and hospitable Arab tribe, after which a delicious Bedouin feast was spread out before us.

Your eye is a lamp
for your body.
A pure eye lets sunshine
into your soul.
– Jesus (Jeshua)
Matthew 6:22 NLT

Sharon took this photo of me taking the backlit photo of Zorg's eye.

Camels in the Negev desert.

Sharon rode with me through the desert, and I enjoyed her company. When taking photos on my own, I often place my riderless horses in the scenery and hope they won't charge off without me, so it was also great to have a willing assistant!

Her daughter Ronny joined us towards the end of the day, and we took turns walking and riding as we travelled to the Desert Shanti village – a beautiful oasis, and such a contrast to the ramshackle, sprawling settlements that we had passed. Entering through security gates, we found ourselves in a world of high quality design, neat paving edged with date trees, and well-lit, tidy stables, designed to allow the breeze to flow through and cool the horses.

Sharon introduced me to Raz Arbel, who gave me a tour of the attractive village, with its impressive, warm coloured Mexican and Moroccan architecture. He explained the concept behind the Shanti House Project, which uses environmentally-friendly materials, water recycling and solar power.

"Some come here as a last resort. A one-time opportunity for rehabilitation, and to start again after living on the streets," he explained, as we strolled along perfectly paved walkways, between rows of date trees lit with spotlights. He said there were thousands of children and youths at risk, who had been forced to leave their homes due to neglect, abuse and violence. Here, they found therapeutic horse riding, agriculture, hydrotherapy and opportunities to get involved in social activities. In the wider community to the south, they had access to schools, hospitals, community services and youth employment.

I relished my beautiful, spacious room with en suite bathroom, and a view of my horses in their smart corrals. The Shanti House charity was an inspiration to me and my own evolving vision to use Dartmoor ponies to work with disadvantaged children.

"See? You couldn't have ridden this section on your own," Sharon remarked, as she transported us in a trailer lent to us by Desert Shanti village. We were crossing a sun-scorched landscape and dropping down to the shores of the Dead Sea, which is 1,412ft (430m) below sea level – the lowest point on land and also one of the hottest, with water that is over nine times saltier than the ocean. Shielded by the Judean Mountains to the west, rainfall is very scarce, with two to four inches (50-100mm) falling in an entire year. The river Jordan is the only major water source, and parts of the shore are closed off due to huge sinkholes and subsidence. The Dead Sea is bordered by Jordan on the east and Israel on the west and is 31 miles long and up to nine miles wide (50km by 15km), although it is shrinking rapidly.

We passed high-rise tourist hotels at the southern edge. Tourists flock here to enjoy the heat and float in the salty water – a far cry from a century earlier when this was called the 'valley of death'. ANZAC horsemen camped here in the scorching summer heat of 1918, when it was up to 52 degrees centigrade in the shade. The horseshoes scorched the horses' hooves and had to be removed. To add to their extreme discomfort, there were venomous snakes, scorpions and swarming mosquitoes, which caused malaria.

They stayed to convince Turkish forces that the next big attack would come from here. But then, under cover of darkness, the army moved out and joined their Allies on the coastal plains. Those who remained constructed fake bridges across the Jordan, pitched empty tents and built 15,000 dummy horses using wooden frames covered with horse rugs. Their trick succeeded, and the Allies broke through Turkish defences on the coastal plains. The ANZACs captured Turkish strongholds around the Jordan valley and took Amman, while the rest of the Allies took Damascus. The war finally ended on October 31st 1918, although more deaths were later caused by malaria, and many horses left without their riders.

13. MASADA

We stopped beneath the looming mountain of Masada in the Judean desert, topped by an ancient fortress, looking down on the Judean Desert and the Dead Sea. The first fortifications were built by Jonathan the High Priest in 152 BC. Later, Herod built a winter palace here, with well-stocked storerooms and cisterns which were filled by rainwater, and the Romans then stationed a garrison here. Three narrow winding paths lead up to the fortified gates at the top of this plateau, about 1,300 feet (400m) above sea level.

Masada is one of the most visited sites in Israel and I joined hundreds of tourists queuing for the cable car. It was so claustrophobic inside (someone said they could carry 70 people!) so I was relieved to get out and breathe freely again. At the top, I looked around the extensive plateau with its many ruins, and gazed out to the west across the Judean Desert and to the east to the Dead Sea and into Jordan.

After the Romans destroyed Jerusalem in 70 AD, people fled here and built a synagogue and ritual baths in some of Herod's palaces. Masada became the last rebel stronghold in Judea, so the Roman tenth legion laid siege to the mountain, with 8,000 troops camped around the base. They spent several months building a ramp upon the natural slope to the west, and used this to haul a tower and battering ram up to the castle. In preparation, the rebels tried to support their wall with timbers, but the Romans set this alight. As their hopes dwindled, the rebel leader Elazar Ben Yair convinced his 960 followers that it would be better to take their own lives than to live in shame as Roman slaves, and they drew lots to decide who would carry out the mass suicide. Today, these Jewish rebels are considered national heroes.

I thought about this heroic and tragic event as I descended the steep, winding path to join Sharon and Ronny. We enjoyed a delicious picnic in the shadow of Masada, washed down by black coffee provided by a horse-friendly gatekeeper. I felt a little sad to say goodbye to Sharon, who had greatly enriched my journey through Israel.

14. THE DEAD SEA

"You fell out of the sky, on me!" Isaac Hanuka remarked, as he drove me and the horses through the checkpoints, into the West Bank and on to Kibbutz Kalia on the northern edge of the Dead Sea.

He pointed to a cliff, high on our left. "See that? It's where the edge of the Dead Sea used to be, but now it's way down to our right. It drops about a metre a year. Israel agreed to give water to Jordan, but a lot just evaporates off the extensive surface. There are plans to bring water from Eilat, with European funding, which will benefit both Jordan and Israel."

The Jordanian, Israeli and Palestinian governments have identified 'Saving the Dead Sea' as a national priority. Ted Beckett, a friend who is involved in the project, informed me, that if water can be brought from the Mediterranean, through a 45 mile (72km) tunnel, it would provide jobs, and benefit the Jordanians, Palestinians and Israelis. It might also fulfil the prophecy in Ezekiel 47:10: "It shall be that the fisherman will stand by it from Ein Gedi to Ein Eglaim (Ein Tzukim) ... their fish will be the same kinds as the fish of the Great Sea (Mediterranean), exceedingly many."

We arrived in the dark and were met by Hemi, who had kindly lent Isaac the pick-up which towed the horse trailer borrowed from the Manns near Jerusalem.

"People don't realise it is too hot to ride here in the day," said Isaac who manages the stables and provides therapy riding for people from as far away as Jerusalem. "Our arena is 430 metres (825 feet) below sea level and in the summer it is 40 to 42 degrees. I have to water the roof to keep the horses cool. Two years ago it reached 50 to 52 degrees. At that heat even the flies don't come out!" Again, I wondered how the ANZAC soldiers and their horses had survived 100 years ago in the heat of summer, and was thankful I was there in late November.

We spread the map over a table and Isaac got directions over the phone from Haim Mann at Alon, to the east of Jerusalem, where I was aiming for the next day. We talked until midnight about horses and the challenges they face on the edge of the Dead Sea. "I use the minerals to cure the horses' swollen legs. There's magnesium down in the south," added Isaac.

Psalm 91

I slept in the tack room and after my late night, I didn't wake until after 6am. I hurriedly packed up the horses while they ate their grain, knowing we had a long, steep climb ahead – from 825 feet (430m) below sea level, to 2,500 feet (754m) above it, near Jerusalem.

Aren't you afraid?" asked the young soldier at the gate, with a gun slung over his shoulder, as I left the security of the kibbutz and rode out into the West Bank.

"In God I trust," I replied. Without God 's protection, I would never ride across the West Bank on my own. I had never ridden in such a country of conflict, but throughout my life I had been blessed with God's goodness and protection, and I knew that whatever assignment He gave me, He and His angels would protect me. When I was riding from Mexico to Canada, a prophet I had never met before told me he saw angels over my head. "When God made you, it's as if He had to make an extra stretch of angels, as you have such an active life and are going into areas of danger," he told me. "God's angels will accompany you, and protect you, and see the assignment is done." I believe this to be true for all my God-given assignments.

I left the kibbutz, with its walls topped with rolls of barbed wire. As was my habit every morning, I recited from Psalm 91 as I rode:

"I who dwell in the secret place of the Most High, shall remain stable and fixed under the shadow of the Almighty (whose power no foe can withstand). I will say of the Lord, "He is my Refuge and my Fortress, my God; on Him I lean and rely, and in Him I confidently trust." There shall no evil befall me, nor any plague or calamity come near my tent. For He will give His angels especial charge over me to accompany and defend and preserve me in all my ways (of obedience and service)." (Psalm 91: 1-2, 10-11 AMP).

15. The Judean Desert

I followed the route that Isaac had marked on my map the previous evening. It took me along a track, into the huge Wadi Og ravine, and out the other side towards Jericho. My heart sank as I saw the busy roads of Almog and the urban sprawl of Jericho ahead, and I whispered a prayer. With renewed resolve, I pushed the horses on, keeping them focused on going forwards and trying to avoid them shying at the donkeys and camels hanging around at the Almog junction.

I was keeping to the edge of the road when several jeeps pulled up alongside me, their engines idling. Feeling uncomfortable, I took a detour through a plantation, only to find it was bordered by a deep ditch. An Arab man who was watching urged us to jump, but the horses wouldn't go anywhere near it, so I had to backtrack. I turned the horses up a steep hill, hoping we could somehow cross a large water pipe which lay ahead.

We made it, and arrived at a road… only to hear the jeeps nearby. I pushed the horses into a trot, praying they wouldn't follow us up the narrow, isolated canyon ahead. The horses were sweating and breathing heavily as we climbed up the twisting road, with high slopes on either side. Only when I could no longer hear the engines did I relax. With a sigh of relief, I dismounted and led the puffing horses. This was the winter, and we were all sweating – I couldn't imagine how unbearable the heat must be in the summer.

The track levelled off and split in several directions across the desert ahead. I examined the map, but couldn't work out which one to take, so I asked some men working in a high fenced enclosure.

"A woman with two horses, I must be dreaming! But you are real!" said one of the men, introducing himself as Roi Natan. "Do your horses need water?"

"Do you have enough?" I asked – I could only guess they would have a few water bottles in the back of their pick-up, and my horses were thirsty.

"We are the water board!" replied his companion, Netanel. I laughed with relief – I couldn't have met anyone better. I pulled out my water bag, and they kept refilling it until the horses had drunk enough. Afterwards, we examined the map and agreed which track to follow across the desert up to Jerusalem.

Fifty per cent of Israel's natural water resources come from the 'mountain aquifer', an underground layer of rock. The rain trickles down from Judea and Samaria and flows into groundwater reservoirs under the coastal plain. Whoever controls these mountain areas, controls the water resources. The Sea of Galilee (Lake Kinneret) is their main water source and due to much of Israel being desert and with a growing population, large amounts of water from the Mediterranean are now being desalinated.

Passing by army bunkers

It really was amazing to be riding through the barren Judean desert, passing old military bunkers and gazing down on Jericho city to the east. I studied the map carefully to make sure I kept to the right track and didn't get lost in the desert.

This was known as Area A, as Dani Gold had explained to me – an area under Palestinian control, which the Israeli forces will not enter unless there is a crisis. Ninety-five per cent of the Arab population in Judea and Samaria live in Areas A and B, governed by the Palestinian Authority (PA). They vote in local elections and pay taxes to the PA, which has its own educational, legal, medical and social welfare systems.

Despite its desert climate, Jericho (the 'city of palm trees') was a famous retreat. Herod had a winter palace here, overlooking the plains, with an aqueduct and lush gardens, growing dates and spices. The Crusaders came to Jericho and in WW1 the British built fortresses here and rigged the bridges with explosives in preparation for a possible invasion by German allied forces.

After a long climb we stopped and looked back down through the dusty haze to Jericho, I thought of the Bible story about Joshua, who led the Israelites across the Jordan. As he approached Jericho, an angel appeared and said, "as Commander of the army of the Lord I have now come." The Lord told Joshua that He had given them Jericho – then a huge fortified city, with a double wall that was up to 25 feet (7m) high, and guarded by a massive stone tower.

God instructed them to march around the city for six days, with priests carrying seven ram's horn trumpets and the ark of the covenant. On the seventh day, they were to march around the city seven times. When the priests blew the horns, the people were to give a great shout, the walls would fall, and they were to run in and take the city. Joshua and the Israelites obeyed, and it happened exactly as God had said.

And the seventh time it happened the priest blew the trumpets, that Joshua said to the people;
"Shout for the Lord has given you the city!" So the people shouted when the priests blew the trumpets...
and the people shouted with a great shout, that the walls fell down flat. Joshua 6:16-20

16. Wadi Qelt

The main route from Jericho to Jerusalem passed through Wadi Qelt – the same road taken by David when he fled Jerusalem after his son Absalom (Avshalom) had made himself king (2 Samuel 15:23), and by King Zedekiah when escaping from Nebuchadnezzar's troops (2 Kings 25:1-6).

It was here that Jesus healed blind Bartimaeus, as he left Jericho to walk to Jerusalem (Mark 10:46 to 11:1). It may also be the place where Jesus told the parable of the good Samaritan (Luke 10:25), as there are so many twists and turns, making it easy for thieves to pounce on travellers and make a quick escape.

During certain Jewish festivals, thousands of people passed along this route to Jerusalem's Temple, following in the footsteps of countless traders, travellers and armies – including the 10th Roman Legion who marched this way to destroy Jerusalem in 70 AD.

I had almost completed my climb when I saw a cross, indicating that a monastery was nearby. I breathed a sigh of relief, knowing I was on the right track. As I led the horses down the steep descent, I was overtaken at speed by two young boys on a little donkey.

St George's Monastery

When I reached the cross, I was hailed by a guide, surrounded by tourists, excitedly waving. "You are the girl I saw at Masada! I thought you were in costume, but you are real!"

I could see Saint George Monastery, clinging to a cliff face below me. It is one of the oldest, originally built in the fourth century by monks who believed that this is where God instructed the prophet Elijah to stay: "God told Elijah to hide by the brook Cherith, which flows into the Jordan River and the ravens brought him bread and meat in the morning and evening and he drank from the brook." (1 Kings 17:5-6)

It was destroyed by the Persians, rebuilt by the Crusaders, but fell derelict until a Greek monk, Kalinikos, restored it to its former glory. It remained in the hands of Greek monks, including Father Germanos, who was famous for his hospitality, but was sadly murdered by terrorists in 2001.

As I was taking photos, a Bedouin offered to look after my horses while I visited the monastery. I thanked him, but declined and remounted to head for my next rendezvous.

Do not take life too seriously; you will never get out of it alive.
- Elbert Hubbard

I followed the narrow winding road, listening out for the big tour buses so I could find a space to tuck my horses away and allow them to pass. I arrived at the place where I was due to meet Haim Mann, who was riding from the opposite direction. While I waited, some Bedouin offered me a very sweet cup of tea and another tried to sell me a belt – but then a tour bus arrived and diverted their persistent attention.

I saw a horseman approaching at speed, followed by a plume of dust. Haim was riding a bay horse with a big star and wore a big smile. This gregarious man instantly dissolved all my preconceptions that lawyers were formal, serious people!

I could not at any age, be content to take my place
in the corner by the fireside and simply look on.
Life was meant to be lived.
Curiosity must be kept alive.
~ Eleanor Roosevelt

As I followed Haim, I noticed he also wore a gun strapped to his belt. We slid down steep desert slopes, plunging into Wadi Qelt, and several times I held my breath, hoping Zorg and Sussita wouldn't fall over the rocks. It was an exciting ride in terrain I had never experienced before. Haim pointed to an old acqueduct which once channelled water to Herod's palace in Jericho, but we didn't have time to linger. The sun had already dipped behind the mountains and we needed to cover a lot of rough ground before darkness engulfed us.

The ride had been exhilarating, and was even more fun because I didn't have my head in a map, planning the route ahead. Instead I could absorb myself in the dramatic scenery and take photographs of Haim and the horses. Sussita wasn't keen to be led by Haim from his horse, but once I remounted she was eager to follow and both she and Zorg proved to be surefooted in the rough, rocky terrain. The sound of their hooves, clattering on the rocks, echoed off the walls of the wadi.

"You see? The desert is very alive!" said Haim, pointing out gazelle, foxes, hyrax, wild pigs and wild chickens. He gesticulated towards rock formations as he enthusiastically led the way on his nimble horse. We passed along ledges into Nahal Hyena ('Tzavoa' in Hebrew or 'Daba' in Arabic) – one of them too narrow for a packhorse, so we had to go the long way round.

As dusk fell, I saw a wolf-like creature with stripes run along the side of the hill and dart into a cave. Was this a hyena, who had been feasting on the rotting carcass of a camel that we passed shortly afterwards? I had to breathe through my mouth to cope with the stench. It was dark by the time we climbed out of the Wadi and reached Alon, where Haim, his wife Ruthy and children lived.

Ruthy and her eldest son Lotem riding near their horse farm.

"It's the smallest riding school in Israel!" said Ruthy, introducing me to the stables and her menagerie. "When I was young like Ronny (her pretty daughter) I built farms with Lego, so this is a childhood dream come true for me!" Ruthy ran therapeutic riding stables with several part time instructors, offering rides across the spectacular Judean Desert.

Haim had to leave the country on business, and although Ruthy was happy to take the horses into Jerusalem, she also had a little baby to care for. The combination of security, traffic and political unrest meant this was going to be a challenge, so they asked their good friend Yossi Levi to help.

"We are sleeping back to back" is how Yossi described his friendship with Haim. "We have ridden all over Europe together!"

Yossi spoke to the municipality to try and get permission for me and my horses to go into Jerusalem. "They didn't agree, but they didn't disagree."

"You will be waiting for ever!" said Ruthy. "They didn't say no, so consider it a yes!"

I set My rainbow in the cloud, and it shall be for the sign of the covenant between Me and the earth.

It shall be when I bring a cloud over the earth, that the rainbow shall be seen in the cloud;

and I will remember my covenant which is between Me and you and every creature of all flesh. Genesis 9:12

A few days before I intended to take the horses into Jerusalem, a friend warned me of some potential trouble: "President Trump has declared he is intending to move the American embassy to Jerusalem, honouring Jerusalem as the capital of Israel." This decision sparked protests across the Muslim world. So with some trepidation, I caught a bus into Jerusalem to see if I might get my horses through the very same gate where General Lord Allenby had passed 100 years previously, as he and the Allied forces liberated Jerusalem from 400 years of Ottoman rule.

17. JERUSALEM

Seeing the old city walls took me back to my first time in Jerusalem, when I was just 19. I made my way to the Jaffa gate and examined the flagstones, which were as smooth and shiny as ice after centuries of wear – I was very worried that my horses would slip and fall. I was also concerned about the security guards. Would they allow me to be there? And what about the risk of protests and unrest?

Jerusalem is the most controversial city in the world. Many believe the trouble began when Israel recaptured its 3,000-year-old capital in 1967, but the conflict goes back so much further. Over the centuries Jerusalem has been attacked 52 times, captured and recaptured 44 times, besieged 23 times and destroyed twice. King David prophesied a time when the whole world would be fighting over Jerusalem (Psalm 2).

We know from the Bible and from archaeological evidence that Jerusalem was established by King David as the capital of Israel in about 1003 BC. He moved his capital from Hebron, in Judah, to unite the tribes of Israel, and to benefit from the endless supply of water beneath the city. David was only able to conquer this almost impenetrable, walled city when his commander Joab used a water tunnel to gain access. David's son, King Solomon, commissioned the building of the First Temple about 40 years later.

The Babylonians occupied Jerusalem in 586 BC, destroying the temple and sending the Jews into exile. In 30 AD, Jesus Christ was crucified here and as He had prophesied, the city was burned to the ground in 70 AD by Titus of Rome. Emperor Hadrian then decided to rebuild the city, in 130 AD, dedicating it to Jupiter. The Jews revolted, were conquered and expelled from the city along with the Christians.

As I stood here contemplating the past, I could sense trouble in the incense-laden air. The army was there in force, gathered on almost every street corner, and patrolling past closely-packed shops in dark, winding alleyways.

"You can't go there today," said an armed guard. He motioned me aside as a stream of Muslims passed by, some jeering at the soldiers, heading for the Temple Mount to celebrate their holy day. He directed me in a different direction, and I followed more winding streets, eventually finding my way out of the Muslim Quarter through the Damascus Gate. Here too, the security forces were on high alert, watching a bustling crowd of vendors and buyers, as more people poured in and out of the gate. Sharp shooters were positioned on the city walls, and international news cameras stood by, expecting trouble.

My attention was distracted from demonstrators shouting on the steps, by the powerful and beautiful black Friesian horses used by the security forces. Their riders reminded me of the knights of old, on their brave chargers, beside the walls of the Old City.

Jerusalem is one of the oldest cities in the world, and considered holy by three major Abrahamic religions: Judaism, Christianity and Islam. The city walls were rebuilt around Jerusalem in 1538 and today they define the Old City, which is traditionally divided into four quarters, known since the early 19th century as the Armenian, Christian, Jewish and Muslim Quarters.

After wandering the earth for 1,900 years, the Jews survived their exile. Against all odds, despite genocides and expulsions, they emerged from the ashes of the Holocaust to rebuild their ancient homeland – just as the prophets foretold in Amos (9:15): "I will plant Israel in their own land, never again to be uprooted from the land I have given them, says the Lord your God." And in Isaiah (11:12): "He shall set up an ensign for the nations, and shall assemble the outcasts of Israel, and gather together the dispersed of Judah from the four corners of the earth."

Despite gaining statehood in 1948, Jordan seized the Old City of Jerusalem, forcing Jews out of their homes and from the Jewish Quarter adjacent to the Western Wall of Jerusalem. They destroyed 50 synagogues and attempted to remove every historical connection to Israel. However, during the Six Day War in 1967, Israeli soldiers had a mission to rescue soldiers stationed on Mount Scorpius. In doing so, they took the east of Jerusalem, which was back under Jewish control for the first time in nearly 1,900 years.

The Western Wall is the last remnant of the Holy Temple, which was situated on the same Temple Mount as the Muslim Dome is today, and destroyed in 70 AD by the Roman Legions. Due to entry restrictions, the Western Wall is the next holiest place where Jews are permitted to pray, and they come here from all over the world. Many pilgrims write requests to God on paper and stick them in the cracks between the stones. I ignorantly walked into the men's section, and was redirected to the women's side, where I too laid my hand on the wall and said my own prayer.

My eye was caught by the shadows of the ultra-orthodox Jews, cast against the ancient stones of the Old City wall, as they marched purposefully on the eve of Shabbat (sundown on Friday). I was curious about their traditions, and later, while sharing a special Shabbat meal with Ruthy and Haim's family, I asked them to tell me more.

"The ultra-orthodox Jews have three closed groups – the Haredi, Yemenite, and Hasidic – and they don't always agree with each other," Ruthie explained. I learnt that their fur hat was called a shtreimel, and was worn by married Haredi Jews on Shabbat and other Jewish celebrations. The long, curled hair falling over their ears were called payots, and were based on a Biblical rule against shaving the 'corners' of one's head. The skullcaps, usually made out of cloth and worn by most Jewish men, were called a kippa, and acted as a constant reminder that God is above us.

An ultra-orthodox Jew wearing a shtreimel.

Men marching to their Shabbat destinations.

A woman praying by the Western Wall.

"It's risky, so why do it?" asked Yossi's wife. "Because I want to!" Yossi told her, "I want to help."

Yossi's parents came from Bulgaria in 1948 and they set up a shop in Jerusalem. Yossi has worked in logistics for the roads, bridges and railway and trains.

"I know every inch of the Old City," he stated, so I was grateful he was willing to take the risk to get us into and out of Jerusalem.

"On Friday there could be trouble in the Muslim quarter," he added cautiously, "but as the Jaffa gate is in the Christian quarter, I think it will be quiet at first light on Sunday morning."

18. JAFFA GATE

My heart was beating fast as Yossi helped me get the horses across the main highway to the ramp leading up to the Old City. As I rode towards the Jaffa Gate, I prayed that our way wouldn't be barred by army, police or by anyone else who could cause trouble or hurt. I was also thinking of those slippery flagstones, worn smooth over thousands of years.

"What you said was true!" exclaimed a man who had tried to sell me some jewellery the previous day, when he saw us arrive.

I dismounted at the gate to lead Zorg and Sussita, who started slipping, and frantically tried to regain their footing on the ice-like stone. "Oh God, angels, help!" I whispered, and reassured the horses until we had passed through, where I breathed a sigh of relief. Immediately the police were upon me.

"You can't come in here with horses," they stated.

"But I've ridden these horses around Israel. I'm British!" I blurted out, and in the next breath: "One hundred years ago, General Lord Allenby came through this gate to declare the liberation of Jerusalem. I will only be ten minutes!" They consented, but said I had to remain in that area.

Lord Allenby was a devout Christian, and probably well aware of the prophesy written 2,700 years earlier in the book of Isaiah (31:5) "Like birds flying about, so will the Lord of Hosts defend Jerusalem. He will also deliver it, pass over it and preserve it." He used two Royal Flying Corps planes to drop 'surrender' leaflets in the ancient city, and the Muslims did as he asked – some say they were inspired by the fact that his signature was similar to Arabic script for the prophet Mohammed. Miraculously Jerusalem surrendered without a shot being fired.

General Lord Allenby, accompanied by the 53 Welsh Division and the West Australians, arrived at the Jaffa Gate on 11th December 1917. Allenby dismounted and walked through the Gate to mark the official liberation. "It does not behove me, a Christian, to enter the City of my Messiah mounted," he said. By then, over 15,000 British soldiers and 2,000 ANZAC soldiers had given their lives to end four centuries of Ottoman rule.

During the previous century a group of Christian Evangelical leaders, including William Wilberforce (who dedicated his life to abolish slavery), had stated that it was God's purpose for the Jews to have their own homeland. In 1917, the Balfour Declaration confirmed Great Britain's support, stating: "His Majesty's Government views with favour the establishment in Palestine of a national home for the Jewish people."

19. The Mount of Olives and Mount Scopius

Outside the Jaffa Gate with Yossi Levi.

Tracey photographing eastwards from Mount Scopius.

Those first steps into Jerusalem by Lord Allenby paved the way for the creation of the modern state of Israel – led by the League of Nations, and later by the United Nations. At the San Remo Conference in 1920, the Principal Allied Powers gave Great Britain a mandate to implement this goal.

However, in 1922, following Arab riots, British Colonial Secretary Winston Churchill published a White Paper, dividing the region into east and west and retreating from that initial goal of creating a wholly Jewish Palestine. Three quarters of the land, east of the Jordan, was renamed Transjordan and given to Emir Abdullah, and the remainder, west of the Jordan, was allocated to the Jewish people. Today's Israel is therefore a quarter of the size of the territory set out in the 1920s.

As Yossi drove the horses in the trailer up to Mount Scopus, north of the Mount of Olives, he said in his usual calm manner: "It's okay. If we'd been seen by any groups of Arabs, it might not have been okay, but we're fine." He added intently: "There's always trouble between the Jews and Arabs. You don't want to take a wrong turning in this area."

I was very grateful for his knowledge of the city, and the risks he was prepared to take to get me and the horses into and out of Jerusalem.

If God can inspire me to believe it,
He can help me to achieve it.
- Robert Schuller

Then I saw heaven opened, and behold, a white horse! The one sitting on it is called Faithful and True,
and in righteousness he judges and makes war. Revelation 19:11

This was a momentous occasion for me, as I was once again in Jerusalem, overlooking the Old City, but this time on horseback! I was just 19 when I first came here, after hitch hiking to Jerusalem. I was back where I made the most important decision of my life, and asked Jesus to forgive my sins and invited him into my heart.

God sent Jesus (Jeshua) his only Son to be the ultimate sacrifice for the sins of the world. He was crucified not far from here, on a hill called Calvary and in three days He rose from the dead. Many Bible prophesies, over thousands of years, had foretold His coming, life, death, resurrection and His return – this time not meekly riding a donkey, but with all His angels, on a fiery white charger, bringing judgement.

For me, Jerusalem was therefore a fitting climax, and the finale to my seven long journeys on horseback. My personal pilgrimage had come full circle, and decades after my first visit, I had achieved what God put on my heart: to ride by faith around Israel.

EPILOGUE

"You must be grateful to God!" Yossi told me, as I thanked him for making it possible to finish my ride in Jerusalem.

He transported us back to his stables on the west of Jerusalem, and the next day I descended the western slopes, which were clothed in beautiful green trees – such a refreshing contrast to the barren desert on the eastern side.

As I slowly zig-zagged down the mountain I pondered on my journey through Israel. It was a short ride compared with most of my other long distance journeys on horseback, but so full, so packed with challenges, so many layers of history and such political complexity. I had also been struck by the amazing hospitality – especially from the Israeli horsemen and women who had created a chain of care for me and my horses, helping me to fulfil my journey.

"Aren't you afraid?" I had been asked that question many times, and was asked again by an older man as I passed through a village. I told him I trusted in God.

"Some Jewish people have a hard time believing in God... after six million of us died in the holocaust," he stated blankly.

"I am so sorry." My reply seemed so inadequate. These people had suffered so much, but I was lost for words.

"It's not your fault," he replied.

As I rode on, I met another old man. He introduced himself as Yehudia and gave me water for my horses and a bagful of oranges. I was once again amazed at the Jewish people's hospitality. Although they had suffered so much, and were still condemned by many people, I had personally found them to be among the most caring and generous people I had ever met.

I returned to Moshe and Sharon Francho's farm. That evening, some of my Israeli friends came to say goodbye, including Sharon Keiran, and Dani and Vivi Gold.

The next day, it was my turn to say goodbye to Zorg and Sussita. These two horses had been so faithful. At first it was a struggle getting them past obstacles as they hadn't been ridden for several years, but soon we were camping out in the Golan Heights with heavy machine gun fire nearby and within six weeks we were crossing Jerusalem streets packed with traffic. They had been incredible, and when Moshe and Sharon kindly dropped them back to their home I had to brace myself – I feared it would be an emotional moment. Fortunately perhaps, it had to be a hurried goodbye as I needed to rush to catch the train.

My mind was taken off the horses as Moshe drove the pick-up and trailer to the station. Sharon helped me cram all my horse equipment into two suitcases, and what couldn't fit inside we strapped to the outside and I staggered onto the train with my saddle bags over my shoulders. As I flopped into a seat, and the train sped north, it almost felt like a dream...

The Lord is my strength, my personal bravery and my invincible army. - Habakkuk 3:19 Amp